Before

MW01047504

KNEW YOU

Loved Me

Before I
KNEW YOU
Loved Me

M.A.K. Moran

BEFORE I KNEW YOU LOVED ME
© 2008 Mary Anne K. Moran

ISBN-10: 1-897373-42-2
ISBN-13: 978-1-897373-42-2

WORD ALIVE PRESS

Published by Word Alive Press
131 Cordite Road, Winnipeg, MB R3W 1S1
www.wordalivepress.ca

For My Mother, I Honour You

There are those of us that have lived our lives never really seeing the true light of day. We have been imprisoned to a life sentence of sorts, day in and day out struggling to crawl out from under the perpetual shadow of another. This shadow is cast from the one place we're all the most vulnerable and from the people best equipped to crush our spirits and wound us permanently—our families.

I'm not sure when it began, or even how old I was when I first felt the hole in my heart that grew to become a cavern of rejection and, to some extent, a degree of self loathing, but with certainty, I can tell you when it ended. That day God gave me a gift I never expected: the day my mother died...the day I learned the truth.

Table of Contents

Foreword

King David's poetic Psalm of praise in Psalm 139 in the New Century Version begins with the words: "Lord, you have examined me and know all about me. You know when I sit down and when I get up. You know my thoughts before I think them. You know where I go and where I lie down. You know thoroughly everything I do. Lord, even before I say a word, you already know it. You are all around me—in front and in back—and have put your hand on me. Your knowledge is amazing to me; it is more than I can understand."

These words point to the fact that every one of us is a uniquely inspired creation of our Heavenly Father and all creation has purpose beyond what meets the eye. The Crown of Creation, a human life, being the ultimate apple of His eye.

M. A. K.'s (Mary Anne to me) story is a beautiful, living picture of how God is toiling away in the midst of our lives from our very beginning days to our last breaths. Her personal journey literally touches the fabric of our own lives and weaves a tapestry we all can relate to, for, as past legacies of people and events from her own family shaped the reality in which she lived day to day, so the legacy of our families often shape our lives. Her story also reminds us of the biblical truth that not only are we "Sinners," but we have also been "Sinned Against."

Mary Anne's story leaps off the pages in such a beautiful way, not in the fact that she faced incredible painful trials, but that she never let them conquer her and through them she discovered God's amazing grace. The constant tug of God's presence is evident all around her, from her earliest moments as a child to the faithful tug that moved her to drive home on a Mother's Day weekend.

For the past ten years, Mary Anne and her husband, Michael, have faithfully served the Lord in our assembly in all types of incredible ways, best evidenced in their gentle and kind approach to touching the people brought by the Lord in the area of their personal needs. As an over-comer in her own life and having personal first hand knowledge that Jesus walks with you through the dark days as well as the bright days, Mary Anne can empathize in a degree that many find challenging.

As I read and tried to place this woman I thought I knew so well into the drama that unfolded, I found myself connecting and examining my own life. I felt encouraged, remembering that I, too, am loved of God, that He walks with me and that my life can be changed when I allow Him a place to operate in my heart. The truth came alive once again that love, acceptance and forgiveness really do make a difference in peoples lives when they choose to release it, even if it involves those who are the closest and who hurt us the most—our families.

My prayer is that by the time you are finished reading this story you will sense God's hand on your life, working to restore your family relations as greatly as He has done for Mary Anne. May you discover what King David and Mary Anne have discovered: God is all around you—in front and in back—and He has put His hand on you! May you truly be blessed in your comings and goings!

~Rev. James (Jay) Davis
Founding Pastor
Mapleview Community Church
Barrie, Ontario, Canada

Acknowledgements

Acknowledgement hardly seems a large enough word to thank the people who influenced or helped with this book, for they all played a significant role in the final culmination of my thoughts and the drive to bring this to print. They are more like the frame around the picture—the essential touch that accentuates the beauty within.

With the completion of this book, I have come to a new understanding of how deeply grateful I am for God's presence in my life. While writing this, there were times only His supernatural power and the sense of His presence gave me the endurance to continue while reliving the most painful memories of my childhood. He is, and will continue to be, my unending source of love and strength.

My husband, Michael—you truly are the greatest man that ever walked this earth. Your encouragement to follow God's plan for my life proved to further demonstrate your commitment to put Him and me first before your own desires. This book would have never come to fruition without your faith in me. The "real life" parts you played in this story are a testimony to your loving and compassionate heart. Perhaps one day I'll write a book about the world's greatest love story: *"ours."*

My daughters—thank you for writing the last chapter. It is a confirmation of how capable we all are of changing generational hurts into legacies of love. Tracy and Courtney, my *"I Do"* daughters—you were the greatest wedding gift any women could have hoped for. Angela, my "miracle baby"—the value you added to my life on the day you were born is worth more than any treasure ever found. I love the three of you beyond measure!

My grandson, Mackenzie—your love for your grandparents, kind heart and incredible sense of humour are the gifts that keep on giving. During some of the difficult moments I had reliving my past, I simply replayed the message you left on my office line and the joy it gave me seemed to make any difficulties melt away. *Love ya*, which isn't hard, since you're a perfect grandson.

Pastor Jay Davis, my Pastor, my friend—you have taught me more about loving people and holding fast to God's plan for my life than any other spiritual mentor I have known. Your commitment to the vision God placed in your heart for our church and our city continually serves as encouragement to me to never give up when we know God is behind us. The time you took out of your hectic schedule to write the Foreword is further testimony to your commitment to helping others move towards the completion of God's plan in their lives. God Bless you and Jody; I love you both.

Bishop T. D. Jakes—we have never met or even spoken to each other, however your book, *God's Leading Lady,* instilled in me a sense of courage to move out of the shadows and into the light (even after 50). I thank God for the tremendous gift of communication He has given you, and I thank you for your never ceasing encouragement for all women. God Bless You.

Chapter 1
/ In the Beginning...

I ALWAYS LOVED that first sentence in Genesis, "*In the beginning God created . . .*" As a child, I would take out our family Bible, the one that had all the great pictures of angels and Moses parting the Red Sea and the names of relatives filling in the squares of the family tree on the first page—most of whom I had never met, but had made up stories about in my mind. I would read that first chapter and my mind would run wild as I would envision God's hands outstretched, with pieces of the world flowing out from His palms and a smile radiating with love and satisfaction from the accomplishment of a job well done. I would then wonder if God exhibited that same smile every time a new baby was born, because that was also a new beginning, a new creation.

I was the third child born to Norma and Gerry (Jarrod) O'Reilly, and I was the baby. They already had one daughter and had felt the agony of a stillborn child before I came along. It was the 1950s and, for most of my friends, this era brought with it June and Ward Cleaver, Howdy Doody and Lawrence Welk. But for me, it marked the beginning of a series of events that instilled in me a type of rejection that seemed to permeate my every living cell. I began a life that, without God's grace, I am certain would eventually have caused me to self destruct.

MY PARENTS ON THEIR
HOPE-FILLED WEDDING DAY.

I was somewhere between the ages of four and five when I began to realize there was a darkness in our home that was perpetuated by a steady diet of anger and hurt. To the outside world this would seem somewhat impossible. for we came and went like most families around us. My parents worked and my sister babysat me. We visited relatives regularly, entertained occasionally and conducted ourselves in a respectable manner no matter where we were.

We always had food to eat and clean clothes to wear, yet we were starving. Our malnourishment wasn't the result of a lack of food to our bodies; it was from the gradual starvation of our hearts. The ability to feel unconditional love was smothered out by resentment and addiction. This continual deficit of emotional nourishment left us all starving, yet capable of pretending we were perfectly well.

This was a family dynamic that had been "grown" and perpetuated through generations. My parents were born perfect, complete creations of God—that is, until they took their first breaths outside the womb and were caught up in a whirlwind of generational traits and behaviours that would be thrust upon them simply by virtue of becoming the newest additions to their families. This heritage would remain a curse of destruction to all in its path unless someone took a step towards stopping it, the first step towards making a change that would result in a new story, a new beginning for all those who would follow after. Those first steps did finally come, but not without pain, and not without great price.

My father was handsome. He was the type of man women found very attractive: tall, with dark wavy hair, an abundance of charisma and a great sense of humour that made him the center of attention on more than one occasion. He was intelligent, adventurous and had a great appreciation for beautiful music and all types of books.

> *This continual deficit of emotional nourishment left us all starving, yet capable of pretending we were perfectly well ... a family dynamic that had been "grown" and perpetuated through generations.*

Dad came from good Irish and English stock. I never knew my paternal grandfather, and the only stories I remember about him seemed to revolve around his habitual drinking and a severe shortage of money because of it.

Although there seemed to be a lack of endearing qualities where my grandfather was concerned, he obviously had a special spot in his heart for my father, as I frequently heard the tale of how, on the day he died, they found my father's baby booties in his pocket. My father rarely spoke about him, probably because my Dad adored his mother and knew his father had caused her pain and hardship.

My grandmother, whom my Dad always referred to as Annie Doolan, was the type of woman who made you smile whenever you saw her. She had an almost mischievous side to her personality. One thing I know for certain, she had endurance. My Grandpa O'Reilly was her third husband. She had been widowed three times over with seven children under her belt, and I'm certain she was still on the hunt for husband number four right up to the time she left this earth for the pearly gates of Heaven. I remember my father joking one day as he told my grandmother that when she died he was going to have "Still Looking for Number Four" engraved on her headstone. My memories always reflect the ways she loved her family. They loved her, and I know she loved me. I was always anxious to see her or have her come to spend the night. I knew there were no special requirements for her to love me; I merely had to be in her presence to become the light of her life.

One of my favourite childhood memories is of being presented with a baby doll that was accompanied by an entire wardrobe of hand-crocheted outfits. Because my grandmother was so financially strapped, I later learned, she had walked a considerable distance in the cold to the local Salvation Army store to find a doll, then scrubbed it clean and spent hours crocheting dresses, sweaters, booties and bonnets for her from recycled yarn. She named her Tootles and proudly presented her to me on my fourth Christmas. Even at a young age, I sensed the great worth of this gift. The love invested in it still pours into my life all these years later, as every Christmas I take Tootles out of her box, close my eyes, hold her near, and still feel my Grandmother's love.

TOOTLES, STILL PRECIOUS IN THE CRIB MY HUSBAND BUILT FOR HER.

My father seemed to inherit the best and the worst of his parental gene pool. He was loving and humorous; however, the same dark demon of alcoholism that plagued his father also controlled most of his adult years. The combination of these traits made it easy for me to love him and even easier for me to fall into the classic pattern of the child of an alcoholic. These patterns aren't taught, they're just learned. We become pleasers, peacekeepers at any cost— even our own self worth—and we never feel safe or totally secure. These feelings become a part of our makeup like a slow

These feelings become a part of our makeup like a slow malignant evil.

malignant evil. But fortunately, as with other life threatening malignancies, if caught early enough, with treatment and change and God's unending love and grace, they can be removed, leaving us to live long, healthy, happy lives.

My mother was strikingly beautiful, with long, flowing dark hair and a real sense of style. There were times I looked

5

at her and thought how easy it would have been for her to be a movie star. I especially remember the Sundays she would "dress for church" with her Jackie Kennedy type of flair. Her nails would be painted bright red and she often wore what I

thought was a "mystery hat," the type with a head piece that fit snugly to the crown of her head and a veiled section that extended down just past her eyes. I remember people frequently staring at her and commenting on her beauty.

I THOUGHT SHE SHOULD HAVE BEEN A MOVIE STAR

She was the daughter of Italian immigrants and, in comparison to my father's family, we spent considerably more time with my mother's family. I even had the opportunity to spend some time in my very early years with my great-grandfather. He was very popular with all of his great-grandchildren, mainly due to his kind nature and what seemed to be an endless supply of candy in his sweater pockets. We would gather at his feet at the base of a large maroon velvet chair, just waiting for that special smirk under his large white moustache that invariably preceded a candy throw. My grandmother seemed to always be sick, and I have very few, if any memories of close grandmotherly moments with her. She usually spoke Italian and argued with my mother quite frequently. She had raging diabetes and terrible arthritis in her knees. I later learned she suffered from depression, which seemed to render her unable at times to show much affection.

My grandfather was more the focus of everyone's attention. He always seemed to have an unusual awareness of and a type of controlling power over what and who was around him. It was a control I experienced firsthand on several occasions. They were married over fifty years, and my mother was not so much "like them" as she was the accumulation of her experiences having been raised by them.

We attended church every Sunday and spent at least two Sundays a month with all my aunts, uncles and cousins, eating around the table at my maternal grandparents' house. My sister and I attended Catholic school and I certainly prayed daily. But

> *While most children my age were praying for Barbies and bikes, my prayers were to be rescued from the hurt, fear and rejection instilled in our household.*

while most children my age were praying for Barbies and bikes, my prayers were to be rescued from the hurt, fear and rejection instilled in our household.

The heartfelt pain came in layers. Almost like the dressings of a mummy, it would continually wrap itself around me until I began to feel as if I were smothering. And in my attempts to catch my breath, I learned to cope and survive by grasping at the intermittent moments in time that almost made me feel normal, almost made me feel loved.

For a considerable amount of my childhood years, my parents rarely exhibited any real demonstration of love for each other, and if they did, I certainly don't remember. What I do remember is the daily fighting. This usually escalated around the same topics and scenarios: my mother's disgust and loathing of my father's drinking and my father's dislike of what he perceived was my mother's lack of love and understanding towards him. I remember the screaming, swearing and name calling. There were times the rage and anger were so great you were almost able to breathe it in. The grip of intense hostility seemed to be perpetuated by this daily exercise of virulent family dynamics. There was simply no escaping it.

MY BAPTISM.
WE SEEMED LIKE ANY OTHER FAMILY.

I guess we were somewhat of a textbook case alcoholic family. We experienced daily uncertainty, for we never knew whether my dad would be sober or not. He was a bartender, so the source of our financial safeguard was also the fuel for the demon that controlled him. My mother, my sister and I smoothly and unknowingly moved into co-dependency, each of us developing our own coping mechanisms. Yet, to the outside world, we were like most families from that era. You would have to look closer, close enough to see the depth of our darkness, the depth of our despair, the depth of our secrets...

Chapter 2
/ The Division

*T*HE FIRST TIME my cousin asked me why my mother liked my sister more than me, I felt a real sense of being exposed. The realization that the roles of division that dictated our in-house behaviour were not carefully hidden, as I had thought, but were, in fact, visible to the outside world created a mindset that kept me feeling less than adequate compared to those around me. Never once did it occur to me to ask for help or even be aware I needed it.

My sister and I were very different. Although you would generally attribute that to our age difference, that really didn't have much to do with it. By the time I was around four years old I realized there was an emotional barrier neither of us dared to cross, a barrier that held me captive until I reached my fiftieth year. You see, my parents chose to separate us by allegiance; we became pawns in a very dangerous game. I held steadfast with my father, and my sister began a lifelong intensive connection with my mother.

I have thousands of memories that connect me emotionally with my father—not all of them are joyous happy ones, but most of them are. As a young child, I remember spending a considerable amount of time with him. Because he was a bartender, he was often at home with me during the day while my mother was at work. In the morning he would slick down my cowlicks with some water and a little Brylcreem. (Of course, if you lived in the US in the 50's you knew "a little dab will do ya.")

> *My parents chose to separate us by allegiance; we became pawns in a very dangerous game.*

We would watch Bill Kennedy and Merv Griffin in the afternoon and go for walks in the evening. Whenever he was home, he would tuck me in at night and we would talk about our dreams for the future. We even had our own special song. He would cup my face with his very large hands and we would sing, *"I love you, a bushel and a peck, a bushel and a peck and a hug around the neck,"* and he would hug me until it nearly took my breath away. My father was an alcoholic, but that never hindered his show of affection towards me.

There were also times his being hung-over served me well. I remember one day in particular when I was left to his care. He was in a hung-over state and desperately wanted some sleep, so the solution was to give me a ten dollar bill to go to the candy store and boy, did I jump at the opportunity! I clenched that money tight and gleefully headed down to the soda/candy shoppe that was owned by the parents of one of my friends. I can still see the tables with red vinyl-seated chairs and a counter with soda machines and striped straws. The candy choices were endless, not to mention the pop, potato chips, Twinkies and cupcakes. I placed as much as I would be able to carry on the counter and my friend's grandmother gave me a stern look of distrust and quickly queried as to where I received my new found fortune. I proudly told her my father needed to sleep, so he gave me the money to buy *"whatever I wanted."* It was a day I shall never forget. Fortunately, I was able to get home with all those bags and consume most of it before my mother arrived home and flipped. That caused a fight that lasted well after I went to bed.

Yes, I certainly had a connection with my father I didn't share with any other person alive. He was my hero. I loved him and I know for certain he loved me. There were very few times we would pass each other without him showing me some expression of caring or love, be it verbally or physically. Hugs and I love you's were commonplace for us. I thank God this is a ritual I have tried to pass down to my children and grandchildren, and it has become a primary action between my husband and me. All those loving times between my father and me were fruitful and nurturing, but they were, unfortunately, not commonplace between my father and my sister, serving as a catalyst for a lifelong sense of rejection from both my mother and my sister towards me. I felt safe when he was there … but there were times he just wasn't able to be.

With the exception of a short time my sister attended boarding school, I rarely remember looking at my mother and not seeing her and my sister together. I would stare at them talking and sharing, wondering how they became so close. They had a bond, a type of united force, which kept me restrained from entering in. When my father would leave for work, I felt a sense of abandonment and isolation. I would often take my plastic horses or dolls and go under the bed to play. Hours spent behind an armchair placed at an angle in our living room created a safe place out of sight. To this day, I am able to close my eyes and visualize the pattern on the material that chair was covered in. Don't get me wrong, it wasn't as if I had to fear for my safety—I was certain to be fed and had ample clothing and care taken for my person—it was the ever confirmed sense of knowing that I was not part of what *they* shared that I sought refuge from. At times I would "command attention" my way, and was met with comments about being "Daddy's Baby" or given the assurance that Daddy wouldn't be home anytime soon to validate my emotional needs. It was lonely and confusing.

> *Hours spent behind an armchair placed at an angle in our living room created a safe place out of sight.*

As time continued, our "family" state worsened. My parents' fighting escalated and the division of sides followed suit. It's almost unthinkable to imagine that my sister and I shared a bed and yet, growing up, I never remember touching her, physically or emotionally. It's equally as disturbing to think I have no memory of touching my mother either. Those were actions and emotions that seemed to be saved only for my sister.

My sister endured some pretty hefty trauma before I came along, early grief that certainly must have played a part in shaping her thoughts towards me and my father. My parents' marriage hadn't started out under the best of circumstances. My grandparents were not happy my mother had chosen to marry someone who wasn't Italian. In fact, I think that is the primary reason my father spent most of the visits to my grandparents' place sitting on their front porch. After my sister was born, my mother became pregnant again and suffered a ruptured uterus, which resulted in a stillborn baby girl. Then, just two years later, my mother became pregnant with me and spent many months in the hospital trying to avoid a miscarriage until I was born, prematurely. Perhaps that was the reason my sister began to cling so tightly to my mother rather than developing a bond with my father, or perhaps my father's drinking just alienated her. She only seemed comfortable and secure when connected to my mother.

I do remember my sister was unhappy a lot, mostly when my father was at home. It was a sharp contrast to the way I felt. Frequent were the times she would come home from school crying because other children had been teasing her about being overweight. My mother would comfort and console her as I watched from the sidelines. Oh, how I longed for that comfort myself! Why didn't she notice there were times I was hurting too? Why didn't she seem interested in what was happening in my world? Why didn't I measure up to the importance my sister seemed to possess? Why wasn't she able to love me that much also?

My soul was screaming so loudly for her attention that there were times I felt I could hardly breathe. I needed my mother, and she just didn't seem to understand that. The pain of her indifferent rejection was crippling, and my father was not in a position to make things better—at this point in our lives he had no desire to.

> *I have only one "best day ever" memory with my mother.*

I have only one "best day ever" memory with my mother. I was quite young, and a woman my mother worked with had parents that owned a farm. We went there *together* for the entire day. I don't remember special hugs and kisses, but I do remember the unusual attention being lavished on me. Just to think that my mother knew how much I would love this adventure gave me a sense of belonging to her in my own special way. It was relaxing and fun, and there was no interference from fighting my way into her presence from beneath my sister's shadow. I vividly remember being excited to see a pen of newborn baby piglets. My mother wrapped one in a baby blanket and brought it over for me to rock to sleep. It was a moment where I connected with her; it was a moment I felt her heart touch mine. I still frequently look at a picture taken on that day and remember it was my best day ever . . . *with her.* Little did I know I wouldn't have that feeling again for decades—not until God placed His hand on both of us . . . again.

My "best day ever."

-

Chapter 3
/ Deliver Me from Evil

I STARTED A love affair with God at a very early age. When we attended church, each Sunday I was absolutely mesmerized by the scenes on the stained glass windows and the many beautifully painted statues around us. I would sit and fantasize about Heaven and how glorious it must be. It was an environment that made me feel secure. God was real to me and I wanted Him to manifest Himself to me in a visible way. I felt Him touch me deep down in my soul with a beckoning assurance of a greater plan. When I was in His house, everything else I was involved with somehow seemed less important. I had been exposed to His goodness and I basked in it. But then one day my life changed forever—the day I felt an evil claw reach deep into my soul in an attempt to draw me to itself and away from God.

I know the life we were living in our home up until this point was unhealthy and dysfunctional, but no pain I endured there would prepare me for what was waiting. What happened was probably the greatest reason I felt confirmed in the fact that my mother didn't love me. This is difficult and painful to write about, but is necessary for you to realize the depth at which God carries us, and has carried me, my entire life.

My earliest memory of feeling the evil that is able to destroy the inner core of a child's mind and heart was around the age of five. It was a series of memories I blocked out of my mind until my daughter was born and I was in my twenties. I'm not sure why, but my parents had left me with my grandparents for the weekend. I was happy to be there in the peace and quiet, a quiet that would later serve as a terrifying precursor to unthinkable acts.

It was a summer night and I had started to get ready for bed. The usual: bath and pyjamas. The TV was on and I had sat on the floor to watch it. My grandmother had gone to bed early, as she frequently did, and I was in the living room alone with my grandfather. After a few moments, I sensed him moving closer and felt the warmth of his breath on the back of my neck. I sensed something strange but didn't feel alarmed—that is, until his grip around me became so tight it began to hurt and he began to touch me in a manner no grandparent should ever conceive of perpetrating on a grandchild.

I remember feeling confused and terrified. His strength and control over me were well beyond my understanding at that age. I was only five. After what seemed forever, he told me to go to bed. I cried myself to sleep, then awoke very early to get dressed. I went to the living room window and stared out at the streetlight. I felt numb and confused. I stood there for what seemed like hours, waiting for my grandparents to awaken so I would be able to call my parents and have them come to rescue me. In the morning I begged to call home. My grandfather took me by the hand and led me over to the phone. As he handed me the receiver and I looked up into his eyes, I saw it ... it was like looking deep into the pit of hell. It was an evil capable of destroying me and I was afraid. When my mother answered the phone, I told her I wanted them to come and get me and take me home. I wasn't able to tell her why, as my grandfather was listening to every word, and because, sub-

My earliest memory of feeling the evil that is able to destroy the inner core of a child's mind and heart was around the age of five.

consciously, shame and self loathing had already started to set in. By this time I was crying and begging. My mother told me to stop being a baby and they would come to get me the next day. But that would be too late.

These episodes continued each time they left me there and they varied in severity and length. I began to rationalize the reasons why my mother left me with him. It must have been a punishment for not being as good as my sister. Or perhaps just because she really didn't care what was happening. For certain she knew I would never be able to tell my father, because he would likely kill him and then I would never be able to see my dad again.

A day came when I thought they would surely realize what was happening. I had cried in the car all the way to my grandparents' home. I begged and pleaded not to be left there. My father said they would stay until I was asleep, and they would be picking me up the next day. I felt a sense of security in that, so I reluctantly stopped crying. I fell asleep while my parents were there with the ease of knowing my father would protect me.

That feeling of security was exchanged for terror very early the next morning. While it was still dark, I awakened to the feeling of evil permeating the room. I opened my eyes and a sense of terror I hadn't ever experienced before engulfed me. It was paralyzing. My grandfather was there at the end of my bed, and as he moved closer, through the glimmer of a nightlight I saw those eyes again. They truly were the mirror to his soul, a soul that seemed to be controlled by the spirit of a predator whose drive would only be quenched by a depraved hunt and devour type of exercise. I saw the satisfaction on his face as he removed my covers and my life was changed forever. I turned my head so as not to be caught in that gaze and, through my tears, saw a makeshift altar with a statue of Mary and a crucifix that had been set up by my grandmother across the room on the dresser. I wondered if that would save me, but it didn't. I endured an ungodly act at the hands of a man who should have loved me, not hurt me.

After he left my room, I dressed myself and cried on and off from pain and abrasion. I sat and waited on the front porch for my parents to pick me up and take me home. When we arrived home, I got ready for my bath but started to cry because the water was stinging me. When my father asked my mother what was wrong with me, she told him I was wetting myself and not wiping properly and it was causing a problem, possibly an infection.

I had never felt so alone. Did they really not understand what had happened, or were they choosing to ignore it? This was also the first time I questioned if this had actually been somehow my fault. I even felt my father had let me down. It was at this point I began to wrestle with a feeling of worthlessness. I endured my grandfather's predator-like behaviour for the next four years. The fear of being alone with him for even minutes was terrifying. It sowed a seed of self destruction, thus beginning a lifelong search for something or someone that would make me feel that my life really mattered.

For whatever reason, and I'm not sure exactly when, I completely blocked the memory of what happened to me out of my mind for several years. When my grandfather died, we were all summoned to the hospital and informed his kidneys were shutting down. He was in a considerable amount of pain and I thought it odd that I didn't care. I had an underlying feeling that somehow he should be suffering, and I didn't know why. At his funeral, all my mother's family mourned his loss and conversations lent themselves to what a wonderful person he was. I felt numb and confused and I didn't cry; I just wondered why I felt detached. I chalked it up to the fact I wasn't part of "their group" and spent most of the funeral close to my dad. After my daughter was born, one day I was pushing her in a stroller at a mall and an older man came over to see her. When he bent down touch her, the memories of what happened to me came flooding back, and with them, a rebirth of my self-loathing and feelings of inadequacy.

Chapter 4
/ The Self-Perpetuating Prophecy

*H*AVE YOU EVER heard the saying "The more things change, the more they stay the same"? Well, that certainly described our family. One day my mother took me aside to break the news to me that she and my father were getting a divorce. She calmly stated I would be staying with my father and my sister would be going with her. To be honest with you, for a moment I felt a sense of relief, but only until the reality set in that my mother was making the final break from me. I recall wondering, maybe, if I could be as smart as I had heard my sister was, then possibly I would have had some value to her. Perhaps I would be able to make myself worthy enough for her to love me as much as she loved my sister. Well, I accepted my fate and I waited, but that fateful day of divorce never arrived and, to this day, I'm not exactly sure why. We just never talked about it again.

Time went by and our household dynamics seemed to change. The anger had become somehow silent. It was a fearful silence, somewhat like a volcano that you knew for certain had the capability of erupting at any moment. My father dried out and left bartending for a respectable job with Chrysler, but the aftermath of our lives until that point would remain like a disfiguring scar. My parents seemed to tolerate each other and even get along some of the time. Unfortunately, the division amongst us was like a permanently engraved pattern on our souls. It still governed even our new-found interaction towards each other.

> *Time went by and our household dynamics seemed to change. The anger had become somehow silent. It was a fearful silence.*

By the time I was around ten, my father's kidneys completely shut down from years of alcohol abuse and he began kidney dialysis three times a week. This was a terrifying time for me. I continually wrestled with nightmares and the heaviness of thoughts of what would become of me if my father died. Who would ever love as much as he did?

As the next few years unfolded, I was forced to depend more on my mother and sister. This, combined with the stress of my father's being on dialysis, started to affect me. Even though I was fairly popular at school, I continually fought the feeling of being the odd man out. I hung around with what would have been considered the "in" crowd; I was continually trying to prove I was worthy to be with them. I struggled with not being as pretty as they were. All of them were blonde, with nice clothes and disposable income. They seemed to be in a position to choose just which boys would be allowed into "their" presence. Oh, how I wanted to be just like them! Every day I seemed to awake and just exist … from rejection to rejection. I realize now it was my own sense of loathing, shame and isolation within my own family that was causing me to have that continual feeling of not belonging anywhere.

At the age of fifteen, I became acutely aware of just how intelligent my sister was. She had started university and I was told frequently that my educational progress was not coming anywhere close to what she had achieved. If the truth be known, I really wasn't interested in being a scholarly superstar. I was much more interested in whether I was going to be captain of the cheerleading team. I was attending high school in the ghettos of Detroit due to a bussing experiment the government thought would help to integrate schools. Although I was spending time in one of the most depressed areas of Detroit, I somehow felt as if I really belonged there. My new friends understood alcoholism, drug addiction, violence and how dreams were vulnerable to being squashed by outside circumstances. They were like me: victims of prejudices and deep dark secrets.

This was also the first place I gave my heart away to someone I thought would love me. His name was Marcus and he seemed to understand me. We were, I thought, committed to each other, and I believed he would never let me down. Not like my family had. I was a teenage girl dragging around loads of excess baggage. I knew he had a previous girlfriend who was gorgeous (and blonde). Everyone thought she was just the sweetest person you would ever meet and I just couldn't understand why they didn't see her the way I did—a constant threat to my happiness. One day, while driving me home from school, he told me he had decided to go back to her. She was more of what he was interested in. *Sure*, I thought, *he just "can't" love me.* I wasn't as smart as she was, I certainly wasn't as pretty and I had, of course, that already self-perpetuating feeling of self loathing that obviously he now felt also. The feeling of rejection at that moment began to course through my veins and surround my every thought.

I took the bus to the hospital and sought out my father in the dialysis room. He was surprised to see me, and as I wept into his blanket and told him I just wasn't able to take anymore, he just stared at me. How much more rejection could I handle? I asked him why Marcus couldn't love me. I asked when the pain with my mother and sister would stop. He said he understood but there was nothing he was able to do to change things. I just sat there with him and waited to go home. I felt numb and completely empty.

When we arrived home, my father told my mother what had happened and she told him to stop babying me. That was when I made my decision. I would rather die than feel this pain another day. I went into the bathroom, took out the bottle of one hundred 222's and swallowed them. A short while later, I began to hear a deafening ring in my ears and started to collapse on the kitchen floor. My father arose from where he was and spotted the empty bottle. The last thing I remember before passing out was my father proclaiming he would kill my mother if anything happened to me. I awoke to paramedics pumping my stomach and asking me to swallow some ungodly concoction.

As I went to bed that night, my father came into my room and asked me if I knew what I had done. I felt like screaming and asking him if he had any idea what he and my mother had done—or was I angrier at the thoughts of what they hadn't done in my life? Yes, I knew, and I was only sorry it hadn't worked. Death seemed the only doorway to relief. I

> *Death seemed the only doorway to relief.*

knew by the look on his face that my father was hurt and even afraid. He told me I needed to pray and ask God to forgive me. I didn't want God to forgive me; I wanted him to send someone to love me, to make the insanity go away.

I lay there and waited for my mother. Perhaps she would come to comfort me. Would the thought of possibly having lost me make her want to hold me in her arms and tell me she loved me just as much as my sister? Would she tell me I had been wrong in feeling that way all these years? She came to the doorway of my room and told me to be sure and get up and go to school the next day. That was it. I wondered if she was just too devastated to say anything else or if she really did not care. I fell into a deep sleep and awoke to the same ringing and a severe case of nausea, but I didn't dare stay home. I called a friend to pick me up and take me to school.

I had heard that God would not send you more than you could bear, but I was having a hard time believing it at this point. However, as I look back on that day, I realize He heard my prayer and sent someone to give me just enough love that day to make me want to go on. It was the first time in a long time I felt God touch me. As I dragged myself into the girls' washroom to be sick, Sister Elizabeth, my English teacher, followed me. She took me to her office and asked me what was wrong. I told her what had happened, and I saw tears begin to fall from her eyes. She came over to me and held me tightly in her arms. She then told me she had been concerned about me, as I seemed to be moving into a place of darkness during the last semester. She had been reading some of my school essays and was becoming alarmed. I sat there in amazement at the outpouring of deep concern she had. She hardly knew me, yet she seemed to have a sort of compassionate love for me, a non-judgemental, unconditional love. Then she took me upstairs to the convent, helped me into one of her nightgowns and tucked me into her bed. As she knelt next to me, she told me God truly loved me and had a plan for me and that I could just sleep there until I felt better. I stayed there most of the day and left for home with the feeling that God had truly talked to me through her.

> *She hardly knew me, yet she seemed to have a sort of compassionate love for me, a non-judgemental, unconditional love.*

I arrived home and we never discussed the events of the previous day. I realized this was pretty much our pattern. Hurtful, hateful, terrible things happened, and when they were over, we just never discussed them again. It became my mission that day to find a way out. I knew there must be a place out there with a person in it who would love me because I was me. I just wasn't aware that God already did.

Chapter 5
/ Finally a Family

*T*WO MONTHS BEFORE my sixteenth birthday, my parents moved to Windsor, Ontario, Canada. I was now in a different country with no friends. Fortunately, my parents let me finish out school by travelling by bus back and forth to Detroit. My parents seemed happier. Perhaps their lives were more settled now. They were finally in their own home after years of renting, and the hospital was just down the street so my father would be able to walk to dialysis. We seemed to be functioning somewhat like a regular family, with the exception of a few outbursts here and there and the fact that nothing seemed to be resolved or changed between my mother, my sister and myself.

I started working in a store part-time and met David, the brother of one of the nurses from the kidney room. We began to date and seemed to really form a connection. I will never forget the day I went to his home to meet his parents. They had lived in the same house the entire time their children were growing up, and his parents had a very different type of relationship than I had witnessed at any time in my life. I thought I had walked into the living version of "Leave it to Beaver." As time went on, I saw the evidence of a family governed by faith. His mother lived to care for her husband and children, and his father lived to do the same. There was no fighting and all their memories were filled with love and laughter. They were my first exposure to an evangelical faith. We continued dating and I became a real part of their family.

As time progressed, I began to notice my parents' resistance and dislike towards Dave. I now understand some of the feelings they had; however, at the time I just assumed they wanted to keep me from being happy or were perhaps jealous of my love and attraction towards his family. One night, my father challenged me about the fact that David and his family weren't Catholic. He forbade me to ever see him or his family again, and if I did, I would be placed out of my home and never allowed back in. I stood there in disbelief. I wondered why the only person who loved me for certain would not want me to be happy. I made a decision. This was it—finally, the way out.

I remember thinking how unaffected she seemed while watching me make a decision that would be life altering.

I explained the situation to my "new-found family" and the decision was made for me to move in with them. The next day I packed my belongings while only my sister was home. I remember thinking how unaffected she seemed while watching me make a decision that would be life altering. I realize now it was just what we had been taught, or should I say, not taught. She simply didn't know how to love me. I was a stranger to her. We had never connected.

I began my new life with my new family. I just knew it would be perfect. Their household was overflowing with a sense of peace I had never felt. David's mother stayed home, and she arose early to make porridge for breakfast and lunch for the "men" before they left for work. She baked for us, and when we all arrived home at the end of our day, dinner was piping hot on the table. I thought I had died and gone to Heaven.

I began attending church with them and what I witnessed was very different from anything I had seen or felt before. Their faith was actually part of their everyday lives.

I would sometimes awaken early and watch David's dad sitting at the kitchen table, reading earnestly through pages of scripture before eating his breakfast. When he prayed, there was a sense of calm expectance. I began to understand he had a relationship with God I didn't know was possible. It was personal. It was unconditional.

After living with them for awhile, it seemed only natural that David and I should be married. I was only seventeen at the time, so I had to petition the courts to give me permission to be married as a minor. I began this petition with a vengeance, as I would not go back. No one would take them away from me. I went to court and gave the judge a very convincing argument towards achieving my goal. I still remember him asking me a very odd question. He asked me if I was doing this *for* myself or *in spite of* myself. I told him I wanted to be married because of love.

Now I realize it was due to the fact I was unable to love myself and was searching for that one person who would love me in spite of that.

We married and began what I thought would be a perfect life. David's parents were devout Christians and they helped me take my first steps towards a personal relationship with Jesus Christ—for this I will always be grateful. I remember the day I accepted Him into my heart in 1973. As my father-in-law baptized me, I felt a sense of newness, but I continued to struggle afterward with the feeling of not measuring up. I did, however, realize I would now be on a journey of learning just how much God loved me, and little did I know how many times His hand would be upon me.

I was informed, by a phone call from a relative, that I was a disgrace to my family and the Catholic Church and that, as far as they were all concerned, I was dead. I remember hanging up the phone and feeling a multitude of emotions, ranging from rejection to immense anger. How dare they be self-righteous after all they had put me through in my life! Never once did I consider I had caused them pain. Never once did I consider what I had done to them. I was totally immersed in my own pain, not realizing that I was continuing to perpetuate our chaotic, alcoholic, dysfunctional insanity.

It wasn't very long after I was married that one of my relatives died and we were all brought together because of the funeral. When I saw my father, my heart melted. I longed for his approval; I prayed he would love me again. My prayers were answered. He suggested we try to mend our differences and asked if David and I would start to come over to the house. It was a difficult time for all of us, but we managed to get through it.

It was more than I hoped for. I had my father's love back, and my husband's family loved and cared for me. I even managed to convince myself I didn't really need my mother's approval.

I was totally immersed in my own pain, not realizing that I was continuing to perpetuate our chaotic, alcoholic, dysfunctional insanity.

Chapter 6
/ Please, Not Again

*T*WO YEARS AFTER we were married, my husband applied to the Metro Toronto Police Force and was accepted. I was absolutely distraught at the thought of moving that far away from our families. He assured me this was a positive move for our future, so I agreed. Never once did I think my life would be entering another season of darkness and rejection.

To this day, I'm still not certain what happened to perpetuate the changes in our marriage once we moved away. Perhaps it was the new environment or the exposure to the excitement of police work, but slowly and surely changes came. We stopped attending church together. I thought it was the strain we were experiencing because we had decided to begin a family and, even though I was able to get pregnant, it always seemed to end in a miscarriage. I discovered my mother had been taking injections of DES the entire time she was pregnant with me and that this drug was causing devastating effects on the daughters of the women exposed to it. I was told there was a great probability I would never mother a child. In total I had four miscarriages, and a year had gone by since I was able to conceive. I began to fear the doctors were right.

I poured myself into the mission of being the perfect wife. The more I felt Dave moving away from me, the more determined I became. I was Betty Crocker and Martha Stewart all rolled up into one. I also became obsessed with my looks. I would starve myself to stay thin, my waist-length hair was always conditioned and shiny and I prayed daily that God would give me a child, for I was certain that would bring our marriage back to where it needed to be.

I poured myself into the mission of being the perfect wife . . . I was Betty Crocker and Martha Stewart all rolled up into one.

During this time, I formed a friendship with a young woman from church. She came from a family much like my in-laws; however, she had begun a search into spiritual neighbourhoods I had never heard of. She told me about a new charismatic type of church she and her husband were attending on Sunday evenings. She talked in great length about the Holy Spirit and how He would move in great ways in a receptive environment. Little did I know that, years later, I would be spreading the same message to people I would encounter. I confided a lot in her, and she told me my infertility could be altered through prayer and a firm belief that God was able to do a miracle even today. I felt renewed. I had hope. I began seeing a specialist and I prayed and spoke to God as never before. I truly believed, and God in His goodness answered my prayers. Well, some of them: I was pregnant.

When I told my husband, he seemed happy, yet a little reserved. My in-laws were ecstatic and my father was in Toronto for what I thought was a check-up, so I was very excited at the prospect of telling him face to face. You see, he had received a kidney transplant two years previous to this at Toronto Western and was subject to regular check-ups. I went to the hospital and raced to my father's room. As I walked in, he smiled at the sight of my unexpected visit. Through his smile, however, I sensed something might be wrong. "O God," I thought, "please don't let the kidney be rejecting,"—not now when everything seemed to be going right. I told him I had some spectacular news: he was going to be a grandpa. There was an eerie silence. A nurse moved closer and took my hand as my father painfully told me he had terminal cancer and would probably not live long enough to see the baby.

I remember blacking out, and when I came to, I did what we always did when something horrible happened. I stopped talking about it and went on with things. Surely this was a mistake and the doctors would find a way to cure him. God could never be this cruel.

The first three months of my pregnancy were strenuous, to say the least. I began spotting shortly into my pregnancy. This, of course, sent off all sorts of alarms. My doctor tried to reassure me but I felt his lack of confidence in the sustainability of my pregnancy with every word he spoke. I remembered the words my friend had spoken into my life and I knew God had a plan for this baby. Once the spotting stopped, I began to experience uncontrollable nausea and vomiting. It became so extreme that I was drinking anything I was able to get down just to have something in my stomach to bring up. I was hospitalized, and the doctor told me my gall bladder was out of control and they wanted to operate to remove it. He also explained the risks to my pregnancy. I thought and prayed about it, and decided I would not consider putting my baby at risk, choosing rather to endure whatever was needed until after the baby was born. I spent time in and out of the hospital over the next few months and, fortunately, my health stabilized enough to let me go full term.

Along with my health issues, I was suffering the immense pain of watching my father die a slow painful death from cancer. I tried to visit as much as possible; however, the four-hour drive each way to Windsor was also taking a toll on me. During those visits he would frequently ask to see my belly and would give the baby a kiss. I was really fortunate to have had enough time with my father to honestly say, when he died, there was nothing left unsaid between us.

I remember one visit in particular, when he seemed calmer than usual and almost strangely happy. He told me my father-in-law had written him a letter, and after reading it, he had asked my father-in-law to come and see him. I read the letter and realized it was my father-in-law's attempt to make sure Dad really knew Jesus before he died, and through those efforts my father made a solid commitment to Christ. My father began to ask me if I was sure I knew Jesus and why He died for me. He also told me it didn't matter what church I was attending as long as Jesus was the focal point and we were really being taught to believe. When my memories bring me back to that visit, I thank God my father-in-law was bold enough to go out on a limb to be assured my father would enter Heaven when he died. Now I know for certain we will be united one day. I left that visit feeling God had touched both of us in a way I never dreamed would ever be possible with my mother. That feeling sustained me during my father's death when I was seven-and-a-half months pregnant.

After my father's death, I felt a sense of abandonment. The one person I knew loved me for certain had left me. Even though this was not a fate he would have chosen for himself, the fact still remained that he was gone and I was feeling an ever increasing sense of indifference from my husband. I managed to convince myself I was overreacting due to hormone fluctuation. I told myself I should be thankful my husband worked so hard in order to further his career for our family's benefit. When he verbalized degrading statements, I knew I just needed to be a better wife and that would make our lives fall totally into place. After all, once the baby was born, everything would change. I just never fathomed how much it would.

> *After my father's death, I felt a sense of abandonment. The one person I knew loved me for certain had left me.*

I went into labour on April 30th, 1978. Once I arrived at the hospital, however, my contractions stopped, and the decision was made to put me on a drip the next morning at 6 AM. My labour and delivery were long and hard. By midnight on May 1st, the doctor told me they were concerned the baby was going into distress and I would probably have to consider a caesarean section. I was wheeled into an operating room and they decided to try one last time. Unfortunately, my tail bone was broken, but the reward was great—*a baby girl at 12:18 AM on May 2nd.*

When they brought her to me, she nearly took my breath away. This was truly the greatest gift God had ever given me. The pain I was experiencing was just a momentary prerequisite for the joy of the gift I had just received: my miracle baby, the baby they said I would never have. I could hardly wait for my husband to see her. I was concerned and upset to find out they were unable to locate him for a lengthy period of time. I was confused about his whereabouts, that is, until the next day, when it all became painfully clear.

The next day I was totally exhausted and the pain from my tailbone fracture was excruciating. I had started to receive phone calls and visitors and was looking forward to getting some sleep. Near the end of the first visitor time allotment, I was just dozing a little when a young woman entered my room. She spoke my name and asked if she had the right room. I didn't recognize her, but since I was in a hospital that was located in the same division parameter my husband worked in, I assumed she must be from his station.

She proceeded to hand me a gift for the baby while she told me her name, and then, in a cruel, quiet, calculated manner, she said she felt I should know she had been my husband's mistress for a considerable amount of time.

There are simply no words to describe how I felt at that moment. The overwhelming pain was so great I thought my heart would explode. I reached for the bowl on my nightstand as I felt the nausea overtaking me. She tried to help, and as she drew closer, I sensed she had accomplished just what she had come for. I calmly asked her to leave.

After she left, my emotions changed from hurt and betrayal to an all-consuming feeling of panic. Would he leave me? Would he actually turn his back on all his parents had instilled in him? I longed for my father's voice and comforting touch. I certainly wouldn't be able to turn to my mother. Even though we had been "nicer" to each other since my father's death, this humiliation would be more than I would be able to bear. My sister was in a "perfect" marriage at this point and my mother detested my husband and his family. I cried until I could cry no more, and then I made a decision. I would say nothing! We would leave the hospital as a brand new family. I would become the perfect wife and mother and that would solve everything.

Chapter 7
/ Darkness and Defeat

*T*HE NEXT FEW years were filled with immense emotional ups and downs. Fortunately, my daughter gave me a reason to get up in the morning. I poured everything into being the picture-perfect wife and mother, even to the point of accepting behaviour from my husband I should never have stood for. He would be gone for days at a time, but I always accepted his explanations without resistance or complaining. While he was home, I cooked, I cleaned and I waited on his every request. I knew there was competition out there and I needed to be ahead of the game. I allowed myself to be subjected to verbal abuse and degradation, and in some sick manner, deep down thought I might be to blame.

My mother was keeping up an arm's length relationship with me, primarily because she was thrilled to have a grandchild. I still heard the tales of my sister's perfect life and her high status professional achievements. She told me how fortunate I was to be able to stay at home with the baby, as I really wasn't equipped to have any type of career. I didn't dare let her know the secret hell I was living in. I did, however, start to hint to my husband that people were beginning to ask me if he was having an affair. He told me to stop being so stupid and to stop listening to what they had to say.

The day did finally arrive, a few months later, where there was no mistaking that she was still in his life. I had gone to pick up our mail and I came across a letter with her name on the return address. I opened it and read every painful word. She was asking him to finally leave me, as she was tired of waiting around. I tucked the letter into my pocket and waited for him to go to work. I got her number from directory assistance and asked her to meet me. I wanted an opportunity to ask her why she was doing this. When she arrived at my home, I remember thinking how very different she was from me in every way. She was younger than I was and very immature. She came armed with an arsenal of just enough information about their relationship to let me know how deeply they were involved. She even felt compelled to seal her mission by showing me pictures of the two of them vacationing with our best friends. I told her I would never give up my family, and she told me I wouldn't have a choice. She was already in control.

When she left, I called my husband at work and told him to come home immediately. He half chuckled at the other end of the phone, that is, until I calmly but sternly told him if he didn't arrive within the hour he would never see his daughter again. When he arrived, I was sitting in our bed. He stood in the doorway and I asked him to come closer. He hesitated and asked me what I was doing. I simply stared, feeling the type of anger and hatred that compels you to want to cause another person pain because that seems to be the only way to release the gut wrenching hurt that is coursing through your veins and permeating your heart. As he sat next to

> *I simply stared, feeling the type of anger and hatred that compels you to want to cause another person pain.*

me, I seized the opportunity. I reached out as if to draw his arms to me, then midway I grabbed them with strength fuelled by pain and anguish. As my nails dug deeply into his arms, I felt no remorse, only relief. I wanted him to hurt as much as I did. As I stared into his eyes I felt myself losing control to hatred.

I began verbalizing the details of my encounter with "her." I began to sob uncontrollably and asked him why. He told me I was boring and he was ashamed to be seen with me in public. I demanded he never see her again, and if he did, I would leave him. I felt somewhat in control for the first time. But that lasted only a moment. He calmly stepped back, looked me in the eye and asked me exactly where I thought I would go. He said no other man would have me, and my mother certainly wouldn't welcome me with open arms. He completed his verbal assault by stating he would do whatever he wanted and there was nothing I would be able to do about it.

He left, and that morning at 4 AM my phone rang and I heard her voice telling me he was on his way home and to let him know he had left his ID on her nightstand. I felt as if I had fallen into a darkness that was blacker than I ever could have imagined. I wondered why God seemed so silent even though I knew He was there. I endured this agony for a while longer, thinking somehow I would make him love me more, but then one evening, as he was getting ready to go out, I questioned if he was going to see her. He told me not to be so stupid, and I began to cry as he walked out the door. A short while later, as I tucked my daughter into bed, she placed her arms around my neck and hugged me tight as she said, "Mommy, I don't think you're stupid."

I made the decision that night. *It was over.* My daughter would not grow up in the same environment I did. She deserved more—I deserved more.

Chapter 8
/ An Angel at My Door

ONCE WE SEPARATED, David's girlfriend's drive to keep us that way seemed relentless. She kept me informed daily of the intimate details of their relationship. She sent me photos of even their most intimate encounters. She stalked me relentlessly. Her efforts became so aggressive and bizarre I eventually had to call the police to intervene. The situation was brought under control and I was finally on the road to what I had hoped and prayed for—a new life. But that agonizing doubt that seemed to have followed me through my life remained constant. Would anyone really love me? And for how long?

I endured the humiliation of telling my mother and sister what had become of my marriage. I thought perhaps we would form a relationship now that I was on my own. We made an effort, but I was still unable to relate to them in the customary mode of most mothers and sisters. Their bond was impenetrable. I knew they viewed me as an embarrassment. And why not? I was at a state in my life where I felt worthless and alone. I certainly didn't think I deserved happiness, but fortunately for me, God had a different plan. The silence I felt between us was finally being broken. He sent an angel to my door.

The two detectives that were assigned to investigate my complaints about my husband's mistress were both kind and considerate of the state I was in. It was a delicate situation and they handled it with care and compassion. One of the detectives took great time and care to explain as much as he was able about the wire tap on my phone and the other measures they were taking to ensure my safety. He made me feel safe and secure. The times he came to my home to check up on me always left me with a sense of hope for something better. I came to discover he was a fairly new Christian, and in our conversations, I felt his desire to nourish that. I remember thinking how fortunate his wife and children were to have someone like that in their lives. He frequently talked about taking his children to swimming classes and all the fun times they had together. Over the next year, as my life was starting to move forward, he would stop by for coffee and dessert and a chat to see how I was holding up.

I had managed to get a few contracts with restaurants in the area to bake desserts for them and deliver them once a day. This worked perfectly, as it allowed me to work at home and just take Angela with me when I made the deliveries. So, as you can well imagine, there was never a shortage of desserts in my kitchen. I usually began baking around 4:30 AM to get a jump on things before Angela woke up. I began to notice that several times a week a police cruiser would be parked in front of my home at that time. At first I thought this was odd, until I discovered it was the same officer I had grown to be friends with over the past year; when he worked nights he would just take a spin around to "check up on me." This gave me a sense of comfort, even though I felt my days of contact from the "other woman" were over.

My officer friend began stopping in two or three times a week. We would swap stories about our children and laugh at their escapades. I would sit across the table and wonder if I would ever meet and share my life with someone like this. He had an incredible sense of humour, and I felt a compassion from him that came straight from his heart. He certainly loved children and he was so good looking! I wasn't sure if God was allowing me to be tormented or if this was meant to be a sign of hope that there actually were men like this out there. Perhaps he would eventually introduce me to one of his friends.

One morning, while sitting across my table drinking coffee (and, of course, eating dessert again), he leaned forward, a little closer than ever before. With a smile that would melt your heart, he said, "I have enjoyed getting to know you . . . and I really like you a lot, so I was wondering if you would like to go out for lunch with me. You know, a real date, not just talking at your house." My heart stopped for a second. I felt hurt and very betrayed. He knew me and the circumstances of how I had come to be where I was. He told me he was a Christian, so why would he think I would ever entertain the fact of being the "other woman"? I felt myself starting to shake slightly as I tried to hold back my tears.

I mustered all my self control, looked him in the eye and calmly asked the obvious. "What about your wife?"

> I felt myself starting to shake slightly as I tried to hold back my tears. I mustered all my self control, looked him in the eye and calmly asked the obvious. "What about your wife?"

He began to smile and I heard a faint muffled chuckle coming from his chest. I wasn't sure if I should leap for his throat in an attempt to catch him off guard and choke him or if this was some sick joke and I hadn't understood the punch line.

It was then I heard some of the sweetest words ever: "I'm not married, and why would you think I am?"

Why? Well, it was very obvious. He had to be home in time for dinner, and swimming lessons, and baths and all those things most married couples did. And he had never said he wasn't married.

He laughed for a moment, then explained he had been a single dad since before he had met me. He had to be home all those times because he was raising two very young daughters. I knew then that God had sent me my very own Angel. Realistically, I knew he wasn't perfect, but Michael was certainly the closest to perfection I had ever seen.

Chapter 9
/ From Perfect to Perplexed

I REALLY THOUGHT my life would somehow be perfect now. Those awful words that had been spoken over me were now squashed and smothered. They said I would never have more than one child—well, yes, they were right to a certain extent, I never gave birth again—but I have been fortunate enough to mother three daughters. My ex-husband stated no man would ever want me, but now I had someone in my life who loved me with passion and conviction.

We married in May of 1985, and began what has now been more than a twenty-five-year love affair. I'm not sure why we thought we were somehow exempt from any problems people might encounter from blending two families together, but we really thought love would conquer all.

Of course, we were wrong. Tracy and Courtney were not only dealing with rejection and separation issues from their mother but also dealing with a new sister and a stepmother. Even though I had grown to love them immensely and I knew Michael loved Angela, we still had issues. An-

I'm not sure why we thought we were somehow exempt from any problems people might encounter from blending two families together, but we really thought love would conquer all. We were wrong.

gela was now dealing with no longer being the only child and the addition of a new "parental figure" in her life. All of this was exacerbated by my insecurities and the little voice deep down that would remind me that if I wasn't perfect, sooner or later Michael would leave me too. I thank God we had enough sense to seek out counselling. God led us to a spectacular woman named June, who was kind, gentle and very skilled at teaching us how to make our blended family mesh together for years of happiness and love.

Michael had decided that if we were going to spend the rest of our lives together, we should start off on the right foot with my family. I tried to explain that there was no such thing as a "right foot" with my family, but he was de- termined. We packed the children into our car and headed down to Windsor. When we arrived, the first thing my mother did was pull me aside and ask me if I had lost my mind to get involved with another cop. I suspected at that point things might not go as well as expected. My mother had remarried by this time, and we had decided it would be a good idea to clear the air and start our lives as one big happy family. Michael and I sat across the room from my mother, her new husband and my sister. It felt as if I had been led to slaughter. Before I had a chance to get a word out, my mother began to explain to Michael what a horrible child and teenager I had been and how I had turned my back on my faith. She felt compelled to explain in great detail her dislike for Dave and how she resented how secret I had been about my marriage. Her husband asked me why I hadn't been honest about the problems in my marriage, and I told them I just hadn't wanted to hear, "I told you so."

My mother didn't miss a beat. She looked me straight in the eye and said, "Well, I told you so."

I looked at them and began to feel resentment creeping into my heart. After all, their lives weren't perfect either. I also had to listen to the details of what a wonderful daughter my sister was, how she had been a wonderful support to my mother and how special her husband was. Then the real bomb: my sister was pregnant. My only edge up, the only grandchild, would now be gone. Our childhood rivalry would now be perpetuated through a second generation. My mother had an attachment with my sister and now she would have that with her children.

When they stopped talking, Michael (my hero) rose to the occasion. He told them he was very aware of my life circumstances and he was devoted to me for life. We would be married—with or without their approval.

I think they were genuinely surprised at how bold he was, and in some strange way that impressed them. We stayed that night and in the morning we packed our luggage, gathered the children, said our goodbyes and got into the car to leave. After the car doors were closed, Michael looked at me and said, "I am so sorry. I thought you were exaggerating about them." We barely spoke about it again.

I continued to keep in touch with them, but after my sister's baby was born, I became much less important to them.

A short time into our marriage, I began to feel as if I was sliding back into the role of trying to be the perfect wife and mother. I began to read into everything Michael was doing, thinking he was trying to control me. I became suspicious of him every time he left me.

So, I began my quest to "be somebody." I convinced Michael we should open a bake shoppe. After all, my desserts were a huge success and I had expanded to the point of supplying a major hotel in our area, along with restaurants and other coffee shops. We found a great location in a very trendy area and began renovations. Little did he know, however, I viewed this as my business and felt that he didn't need any status in it. He had a wonderful career as a police officer and people revered him. I was the one who was a nobody—or so I thought. We began the venture together but, through no fault of his own, Michael soon found he was unable to work with me, so he stepped back. Our marriage was still very much intact, and we were very happy to be attending church and raising our family together. He just didn't know how much my insecurity and the scars from my past were taking hold. I didn't even realize what was happening.

I became driven by an obsession that was being fuelled by self doubt and insecurity. Michael was unable to help me, but, thank God, he was able to love me. The restaurant was a success, and the one dream I had held onto for years seemed to be coming true.

My family seemed to be noticing me. My mother began to call. She started to talk about me to her friends. I felt as though I was really becoming important to her and this made me feel like a somebody. I had finally accomplished something. I put an enormous amount of effort into making it work and I just couldn't take a chance at losing it; the cost would be devastating. The problem was I wasn't able to do it on my own and I just couldn't bring myself to ask for help. I became so stressed I decided to sell, but I was sure my family would understand. Then it happened—they began to back away and I had to deal with the fact I was no longer a somebody to them. I had gone back to just being me.

> *Michael was unable to help me, but, thank God, he was able to love me.*

During this period I wrestled with my faith. I began to think in very negative terms towards myself. Even though I was able to tell my children how much God loved them, I just wasn't unable to imagine He truly loved me. If I had failed the people around me, then how much more must I have failed Him? I needed to be someone again! I needed to feel important.

Around this time a businessman I had met approached me to see if I wanted to invest in a business. He had a company that made frozen muffin and cookie batter for restaurants, bakeshops, hotels and other types of onsite baking establishments. This was my new chance. I had made money from the sale of the restaurant and would be able to set up a facility close to home to make it convenient. I was off and running and I began the same cycle I started with the restaurant. And, to my delight, my family re-entered my life once again.

I was very inexperienced at business, but my new partner was old enough to be my father and had several other successful businesses. He also owned a muffin shop in a prestigious area of Toronto that sold enormous amounts of muffins and cookies made from our batter. I was moving along with the new business, working hard both mentally and physically. I trusted my partner to look after all the legalities since he was much more experienced at this than I. After a year he approached me with the idea of franchising the muffin/coffee outlet. This was spectacular, or so I thought. I would not only be a success behind the scenes, I would now become an owner in an organization with huge potential.

I was fulfilling a dream with one major downfall—I never asked my husband's advice. I thought I could do it on my own.

My partner had been involved with major construction in Toronto for many years and began to scope out locations. He had franchise lawyers draw up contracts and we began to advertise franchises for sale. I thought I was on my way. Once the first couple of stores were sold, I noticed my partner began to back away from the operation. I noticed how more and more money was being drawn out of the business for "legal" and operational matters I wasn't involved in. I set my concerns aside, though; I was too busy trying to run things and four franchises had been sold. Two of the stores sold were to a woman who was the common-law wife of a police officer in my husband's department, and my sister, her husband and my mother bought the other. Yes, this was what I wanted, finally. I was in contact with my family daily, and they were impressed by what I was doing.

My family's store was the next to be done. I went to Windsor, we signed the agreements, they gave me the down payment and the store began to be built. My brother-in-law assured me they had the funds secured for a loan for the balance and there was enough from the deposit to proceed. My partner began to press me for some of the funds from this location and I started to become uncomfortable with the pressure. When the store was nearly finished, I called my family to tell them we would be signing the final papers and the remainder of the monies would need to be advanced. It was then they told me they had decided to go with a different bank and would need a few more days.

When I arrived in Windsor, my brother-in-law took me aside and began to tell me he had the money but now it was being held up, so he just needed a few more weeks. I told him this was unacceptable, and he begged me not to tell my mother, as it would kill her. I told him I would have to put the franchise back up for sale and he agreed that this would only be a last resort if he was unable to fix the situation. I was absolutely beside myself. How could this be happening? I had told my husband everything was going great, and now this. I decided to go home and call our business lawyer. I was totally unprepared for what I heard next.

I tried for two days to contact my partner and our lawyer. Finally, after several calls the lawyer came on the phone and queried as to what authority I had to call and ask intimate details about the business. I was taken aback and confused. I started to explain that I knew we had not met as of yet, however, I was a partner and felt I had every right to call to ask advice about the next step. There was a moment of silence on the other end. He then boldly asked what would give me the idea I was a partner, for I was only an employee. I quickly began to correct him by stating I had invested in this business and had signed legal documents to become a partner. He said if I had signed papers, he certainly didn't know about it and they couldn't possibly be legal and binding. I hung up the phone and hung my head and sobbed. I realized I had been stupid enough to be taken.

Over the next month, I did whatever I could to try to rectify the situation. I thought somehow I could make it right for everyone concerned. My family's store was built and opened, but my brother-in-law wasn't able to "fix" the situation. I knew I had to confront my mother with what was happening. I called her house and my brother-in-law answered. We argued and yelled about the position he had put me in. I told him I wanted to speak to my mother to see what she had planned to do, and he told me I wouldn't be able to speak to her now or ever, because they wanted nothing to do with me. I started screaming at him, asking him what he had said to her. He simply told me to never have contact with them again and hung up the phone.

I was devastated and began a downward spiral. I managed to get money back to two of the purchasers, but no matter what I tried to do, I wasn't able to make it better. The setback from not being paid for my family's franchise

From Perfect to Perplexed

and the situation with my so-called partner would cause us to go under. I was confronted by the other purchaser and began to receive threats about what would happen to me if they didn't receive their money back. I tried to explain the situation but they just wouldn't listen. I was forced into telling my husband what was happening and he was, of course, devastated as well. Little did he realize what was lying ahead of us. It would be a horrific experience that would test our love, our marriage and, most of all, our faith.

I was being bombarded by calls and accusations. No matter what I tried to explain, no one seemed to listen. Just when I thought the situation couldn't possibly become any worse, I received a visit from the other purchaser and her common-law husband. They were demanding their money back. I tried to explain to them that I had also been taken; however, they said they didn't care. They told me if we didn't pay them back out of our personal funds, he would have me arrested and put in jail for a very long time. "How absolutely ridiculous!" I thought. Even if they did manage to get the police to investigate this, they would simply find out what a crook my partner was. I told them I would not be paying them since I had also been taken, and in a few short months, what I thought was a ridiculous suggestion became a horrific reality. I received a call and was asked to surrender myself to the same department my husband worked for. I was charged with six counts of fraud. I was angry and terrified.

What came next was more than I thought I would be able to bear. Why would God allow this? He knew I was innocent, so why didn't He stop me from being accused and arrested? It was bizarre: how could I be arrested when the police never even came to interview me?

In a few short months, what I thought was a ridiculous suggestion became a horrific reality.

The details of the circumstances that led up to my trial and the events that unfolded during it could fill another book, which someday I may decide to write. However, at this time I will give you a brief overview because it is important that you know that scripture is absolutely true—God will never give you more than you can bear, even though at times it may seem cruel and hopeless. I now know He allowed this because it was a life changing experience for both my husband and me.

The trial was gruelling and humiliating. I even had to endure watching my partner smugly take the stand. Once it hit the papers, so-called friends and even church members turned their backs on us. Because of my financial situation, I was forced to apply for legal aid. This was my first indication that God hadn't abandoned me. I was assigned to one of the best criminal lawyers in Toronto. He told me he would be very surprised if it made it past the "prelim," as the whole thing was preposterous. He was wrong. It was then that he began to question the "outside" influence that was driving this. When we were preparing for trial, my husband went through horrific circumstances at work, yet he never budged in his allegiance and defence of me. I began to wonder just how long he would be able to stick it out.

I was confident in my lawyer's ability and was feeling better about the trial, that is, until the day he called me to say he would be going off on paternity leave and would be giving my case to another lawyer. I couldn't believe it. Who else would be turning their back on me? What I didn't realize at the time was that my new lawyer was perfect for this case. He understood the judge and he believed in me. He also had many years of experience under his belt.

The trial lasted weeks longer than I expected and I thought the judge was extremely bizarre. The worst of it was that Michael wasn't allowed to be in court with me, so I felt extremely alone. I am also saddened to say that only one assistant pastor from the church we were attending came to visit me. Our faith had certainly been challenged during this time, but not without some positive outcomes. Michael had begun reading his Bible daily. We were keeping our family together and doing what we were able to keep afloat financially.

When the day came for the judge's decision, I awoke that morning in a rather strange mood. I had been praying during this time but wasn't feeling particularly connected to God. Our children had gone to school and I was sitting alone in my living room. I looked to the heavens and, for the first time in my life, came boldly before God's throne. I yelled and asked Him why He was allowing me to go through this when I was as much a victim as the rest of them. I demanded to know His plan and what the outcome would be. I needed Him to speak to me NOW. I opened my Bible to 1 Corinthians and read out loud:

I came to you in weakness and fear, and with much trembling. My message and my preaching were not

with wise and persuasive words, but with a demonstration of the Spirit's power, so that your faith might not rest on men's wisdom, but on God's power. [*]

At that moment I understood. I was resting on men's wisdom, not God's power. He was telling me to start putting faith in Him and to stop dwelling on what had happened in my life to this point. He had a plan for me and I needed to stop getting in His way. We left for court and I arrived with a quiet confidence, knowing I had genuinely heard from God.

> *At that moment I understood.*
> *I was resting on men's wisdom, not God's power.*
> *He was telling me to start putting faith in Him . . .*

It was rather strange that in all the previous days I was at court there were many, many curiosity seekers and spectators. It was as if Satan had all his reinforcements there to weaken my spirit. But on this day there was hardly anyone. When the judge entered the room and looked straight into my eyes, I knew everything was going to be all right. He looked around the room and stated he wanted to make some comments before reading his decision. He began by saying how appalled he was that I had been put through this. He glared as he declared that I had been the biggest victim in the whole situation and that my partner was the person they should have been investigating. He also stated he was extremely suspicious of the motives of the policemen involved in the case and what place the whole department played in my witch-hunt. He

---

[*] 1 Corinthians 2:3-5

then ran through the legal charges one by one and at the end of each said, "Not guilty. Not guilty." He then looked at me and said he hoped I would be able to put my life back together.

At that moment we stood while he left, and the courtroom seemed strangely quiet. It was then I heard God tell me to look behind me. I turned and looked at my husband, the man who had stood by me, and realized I had finally found that person who would love me unconditionally *forever*.

Chapter 10
/ The Next Ten Years

*T*HE FOLLOWING YEARS were spent on rebuilding. I had come to a clear realization of the mistakes I had made, and Michael and I were spending time and effort strengthening our relationship. Our children were growing and we were busy working to repair our finances. Both of us had experienced God's grace and, more importantly, His *presence* during our times of struggle. Although we had been Christians for many years by that time, we felt ourselves searching. We had attended a couple of different churches in our area and were absorbing as much information as possible. I felt myself growing closer to God, but continued to struggle with guilt and inadequacy. I am certain during this time God, in His mercy, knew how wounded I was and began to heal me slowly, as my emotions could only take in bits at a time.

Life was moving in a more complete pattern. Opportunities for better jobs began to develop. I had always been interested in health and nutrition, so God put people in my path who would point me in that direction while earning an income doing so. I was enjoying watching my daughters grow into women and was determined my relationship with them would stay strong. I resolved to love them unconditionally, and they certainly tested that resolve on more than one occasion.

One of our greatest discoveries during this time came as a result of our daughter Tracy being married. Her future in-laws were new Christians and they were being baptized at a church in our town. We decided to attend to show our support for them. I had seen many baptisms during my years of attendance in the Evangelical Christian arena, but somehow this seemed different. Although the words being used were familiar, their application was filled with a greater sense of expectancy. I felt the Holy Spirit moving amongst us and joy seemed to permeate even the air we were breathing.

By the time we left that evening, we knew we had found the place we belonged. We began attending and learning more and more as each Sunday passed. During the next months God began to reveal more of His plans for our lives. We made friends and they truly cared for us. God's word tells us He will restore the years that have been taken from us, and that is exactly what started to unfold. We read scripture daily and began to apply its principles to our lives. I felt like I was running at full speed to gather up as much of God as my heart would hold. It was like waking from a spiritual coma and wondering where I had been all those years since I gave Him my heart. It was then I realized that, years before, I gave God my heart but had failed to give Him my life.

God began revealing every manner in which I would be able to serve him wholeheartedly. For instance, I had been a Christian for over twenty years and hadn't even learned the principle of tithing. Of course, this lesson came at a time when money seemed the tightest. Our pastor at that time gave the once-a-year lesson on tithing and offerings. I have to admit that,

> *It was then I realized that, years before, I gave God my heart but had failed to give Him my life.*

previously, I probably would have tuned this topic out or spent a great deal of effort perusing the bulletin; however, this time something was different. I was glued to every word. I heard about blessings and grace and how all God expected was ten percent and He wanted me to have all the rest. I learned that He would take care of all my needs and even bless me some of the times I didn't deserve it. I left feeling special to Him. I was excited.

When we arrived home, I spoke to Michael, and we decided if we were committing our lives fully one-hundred percent, then this was a step of faith we would have to take. It wasn't easy, especially when, right after we put our cheque in the offering plate the next Sunday, an announcement was made that a concert would be taking place the following Sunday evening that both of us would love to attend. The cost was only five dollars per person, but we just didn't have the extra money—*now.* I left feeling somewhat melancholy, especially when a couple that had come with us to church that week expressed their regret at not being able to afford to go either. That night I said my prayers and told God I was still feeling happy and confident in our new decision to tithe, even if it meant not going to the concert. The next morning I went to work early because I needed to get money for groceries before I started. As I entered the mall, it was quiet and it seemed only the security guards and myself were there. I went up to the bank machine, and as I went to put in my card, I glanced down and there was a crisp new twenty dollar bill!

I was elated. We had been faithful, and now God was treating us to the concert with enough to take the other couple. Needless to say, we have tithed ever since; not because we are waiting to see what God will give us, but because it keeps us totally connected to Him. We began to be blessed on a regular basis. One of the greatest blessings God chose to bestow on us during this time was the birth of our grandson, Mackenzie. It was the beginning of a new chapter in the life of our family. He is a gift we shall forever be grateful for.

As time passed, we made the decision to sell our home and downsize. I had mixed feelings, but felt in my heart this was the right decision. We searched out affordable housing in several areas and I strongly voiced my willingness to move out of our area. However, I would *never* agree to move to *Barrie*. Let me be the first to tell you—if you even mention to God you are searching out His life's plan for you, then you have forfeited the right to use the word "never!" We found a wonderful house *in Barrie*.

Of course, now we had to find a church. We had decided to try a couple of the churches in the area before we made a decision. I had heard a church had begun as a result of a vision God had put on the heart of the youth pastor from our previous church. In fact, he was the pastor performing the baptisms that fateful night just a year and a half previous. We went there two days after we moved in, and have now been there for over nine years. I guess we just won't get around to trying out those other churches.

Michael and I decided to commit time and effort to God's people and His church. We became involved with different ministries, made friends and studied our Bibles as never before. We also began to influence and help others who had been through different types of hardships. We learned we had a love and a compassion for people we had never experienced before.

During this time, I learned some great lessons in forgiveness. I knew I had come to the place of God intervening to help me make the decision to forgive my ex-husband. It was difficult, but I had come to an even greater understanding of the part I had played in the downfall of my first marriage. We were too young, and I was searching for someone or something to fill the immense void my heart had felt most of my life. I was in no way excusing him for the way he treated me, but I did learn that forgiveness was a comforting release from the burden of my past hurts. We attended Cleansing Stream Ministries and I was even

> *I was in no way excusing him for the way he treated me, but I did learn that forgiveness was a comforting release from the burden of my past hurts.*

able to forgive my grandfather, an exercise in allowing God to work supernaturally, as I would never had been able to do this of my own free will.

71

I was, however, still haunted by the situation that had occurred with my family. I was angry that my mother hadn't even tried to contact me to find out the truth about the franchise. I knew she had a special bond with my sister but I never imagined she wouldn't be at least curious about what really happened. I tried to contact her by phone and mail several times but was always met with total rejection. After a number of years I just stopped trying.

I become involved with the Divorce Recovery group at our church and they asked me to be the guest speaker at a few of the sessions that dealt with forgiveness. In preparation, I would usually spend time praying for an anointing to touch the people attending that would prompt them to want to forgive their ex-spouses.

One time in particular, I felt slightly restless while preparing to speak. As I prayed and asked the Holy Spirit for guidance, God spoke to me with that still small voice and told me (my own words) I had a lot of nerve speaking to someone else about forgiveness when I hadn't dealt with the forgiveness issue with my mother. I began to argue with God and state my case. Didn't He remember all the times I had tried to contact her? All the phone calls that were met with a loud hang ups in my ear? He kindly but gently reminded me once again of how I was using man's power and not God's power.

I decided to test Him (or maybe deep down I was trying to prove myself right). I went to the phone and dialled my mother's number. It seemed to be taking an eternity to ring. During those moments, I started rehearsing what I would say. I would tell her I had forgiven her for her lack of love and for the rejection I had experienced throughout the years. I would demand she listen to what had transpired ten years before that. Yes, we hadn't spoken in ten years! It was at this point I felt God's presence in a very convicting manner. He was saying "NO. You don't get it. When she answers, you will ask her forgiveness for any time you may have hurt her through the years. This will be the true measure of how your faith has grown and how you have come to know Me, to really know Me." There was no time to think; I had truly heard from Him and now was the time to act on all I had learned through my struggles and growth.

My mother answered and I felt a lump in my throat that rendered me nearly unable to speak. "Mom, it's me…" then a pause. I waited for the usual hang up. There was a moment of silence filled with the anticipation of rejection once again. I said, "Please don't hang up."

At this moment, I waited anxiously for the Holy Spirit to intervene. *Dear God, if you want to shine through me I need Your help, I need Your words.* Then they came.

"I just called because I wanted to say I was sorry for any time I have ever hurt you, and I just wanted to talk." There was more silence, and I waited for the click.

Then it happened. She said she would talk on one condition: that we didn't bring up the past. I agreed, and our new journey began. This time I felt different—this time I felt God in our midst.

Chapter 11
/ Isaiah 41

For I am the Lord your God,
who takes hold of your right hand and says to you,
Do not fear; I will help you.[*]

O H, HOW I loved and leaned on that scripture! I knew if I was venturing into a new relationship with my mother, I would soon be testing my belief in it as well. Ten years had passed and I was different now. I had tried to put the past behind me but now I was dragging it out of the pit I had locked it into. I made the decision to go slowly and test the waters where my mother and sister were concerned. Michael told me he would support me in any way I needed him to, but his concern for my wellbeing was certainly understandable. One of my priorities was to tell my daughters about the reconnection with my family. I wasn't surprised at their mixed emotions, for they had also experienced the sting of my family's rejection. However, as expected, they provided me comfort and support.

---

[*] Isaiah 41:13

I called my mother weekly for the first couple of months. Our conversations usually revolved around the weather, my sister and her children. During one of our early conversations, I felt an uneasiness creeping in. My mother seemed a little distracted, almost saddened. About ten minutes into our chat, she paused and said she had something to tell me but she wasn't sure just how.

Several thoughts passed quickly through my mind. Was she getting ready to tell me she had changed her mind and wanted to end our newly established connection? Would she reject me again?

I decided to take the bull by the horns.

"What's wrong?" I asked, "Don't you want me to call you? Are you sorry we started this?" I was shocked how quickly and loudly she came back at me with a response.

"Oh no! It's not like that at all. Don't stop calling me."

I heard the tone of her voice change to a quiet sternness, shadowed by sadness. "I spoke with your sister, and you need to know she's not happy we're talking and she has absolutely no interest in seeing or speaking to you."

I listened to her words and swallowed deeply. I wasn't entirely sure how I was feeling. That lasted only a moment before an intense overflow of decades of anger began to rumble through my system. I felt tears begin to cascade down my cheeks. It was as if my feelings were so intense, if I hadn't begun to cry, I would have exploded. What was she trying to say? Would my sister's actions once again be the deciding factor that regulated the degree of intensity in which my mother and I would be allowed to interact? NOT THIS TIME. God hadn't brought us to this point only for us to succumb to past behaviour. I decided to take control of the conversation.

God, help me.

"Mom, my sister is entitled to her feelings, but at this point in time I'm only interested in what is happening between you and I. My relationship with you is separate from your relationship with her." This was the first time in my life I had drawn a definitive line between my sister and myself where our mother was concerned. Did she get the undertone to those statements? I was entitled to a relationship with her that was different from "their" bond to each other. I knew this was our last chance.

Then I heard the Holy Spirit say, *Tell her you love her.* What? Oh no, it's too soon. Love me? I'm not sure she even really likes me. I flashed back to my first phone call and knew I had to step out in faith.

"I love you, Mom. I hope you love me too." It was like waiting for a bomb to drop. I closed my eyes and waited.

"Of course I love you," she said, "You came out of my flesh.

> *I felt the start of a purging in my soul.*

You're part of me." She then told me she had made up her mind to keep in contact with me no matter what. We hung up the phone, and as I sat there replaying our conversation in my mind, I began to cry. The crying soon turned to uncontrollable sobbing. I felt the start of a purging in my soul. That purging continued for the next six years. During that time, her words echoed through my thoughts frequently. *You're part of me* ... and for the first time I was feeling affirmed in those words.

After talking back and forth for a couple of months, I decided to take the next step and actually drive down to see her. I was unbelievably nervous. This visit would be different. We were different. I wanted our visual reunion to be special. I was feeling somewhat pleased about us. For the first time in my life, I felt a connection with her. We seemed to be more relaxed with each other. There were no expectations and that relieved a lot of the pressure. I nearly drove myself crazy trying to think of a way to make our meeting exciting and joyous. I wanted her to know all about the person I had now become. I wanted God to be an evident part of my life. Then it hit me. *I'll bring my grandson.* She would be thrilled. They had talked on the phone and he had begun to refer to her as Great-Nana. It would be the perfect icebreaker.

As we arrived at my mother's home, I felt awkward and nervous. I sat in the driveway, contemplating backing out and going back home. Just then I heard my grandson's small voice asking, "Don't you want to get in there and see your mom?"

As I turned to look into his eyes, I saw the smile of anxious anticipation on his face. Little did he know that the answer to that simple question would stand as a prophetic declaration of whether or not the change in generational mother-daughter relations in my family would start with this reconciliation. I looked at him, and with a sweet anticipation of the results from the first steps of change, I said, *"LET'S GET IN THERE!"*

I knocked on the door and heard my mother's voice yell, "Come in." I opened the door, and it was as if time had stood still. She was sitting in her favourite chair, as usual, with a cup of coffee on her side table. "Well, who's this handsome guy?" she asked as we entered.

Mackenzie ran into her arms to give her a hug, exclaiming, "It's me, Great-Nana! Remember? I said I was coming." It took all my strength not to break down. I was witnessing a sight I never expected to see in my lifetime: a connection between my family and my mother.

She then turned her focus and attention to me. "Who's this old lady you brought with you, Mackenzie? She has grey hair." Wow, I thought. I forgot the last time she saw me I had dark hair. Ten years had made a difference to both of us.

Mackenzie turned, and with a stern declaration he announced, "That's my grandma. She used to be your baby." I felt a strange sensation. It was as if he announced a secret that had been hidden until this moment in time, something I had never really spent time or effort thinking about. *I was her baby.* I hadn't just materialized out of thin air to make her life miserable.

Her statement over the phone rang loudly in my head once more. *Of course I love you; you came out of my flesh.* I wondered if that would be the extent of the

> *I was her baby. I hadn't just materialized out of thin air to make her life miserable.*

level of our relationship or if God would take us somewhere we had never been before. I would wait and see.

Just at that moment I had the shock of a lifetime. My sister came around the corner from the kitchen. I didn't know what to say and I think I came up with something profound like, "Hi."

Why are you here? I thought. *I'm not dangerous; my mother doesn't require back-up.* Then all those old feelings came flooding back with a vengeance. It was the two of them together again and I wouldn't be able to penetrate their circle.

All right, I thought. *If we're at the edge of change, than I may as well shock the heck out of everyone.* I took a deep breath, stood up, walked over to my sister and hugged her while I kissed her on the cheek. It was one of those polite embraces, somewhat like the attempt a twelve-year-old boy might make towards a maiden aunt at a family reunion. She sort of nodded and said hello. *Okay, Lord, we need some type of miracle here.* He heard me and He answered. My sister received a phone call to go home to attend to something, so Mackenzie and I had time alone with my mother.

The conversation stayed fairly generic. We talked about family and I showed her pictures of the girls. She seemed really happy to see me. We reminisced about Angela as a baby and I began to see a difference in her. I knew she had begun to look at me in a different light also. I was careful not to push too hard during this visit. She had set limits on what we were to discuss and I respected that. During this visit, I also had the opportunity to see my sister's family and have dinner with all of us together. The interaction was a bit strained, but every time I looked at Mom, she smiled at me with warmth and a look that left me knowing this wouldn't be the last time we would visit.

> *I took a deep breath, stood up, walked over to my sister and hugged her while I kissed her on the cheek.*

After returning home, I felt a mixture of emotions that ran somewhere between joy and a longing sadness. I had a renewed belief in God's ability to heal relationships; however, this wouldn't be so much a healing as it was creating a new a relationship that had never really existed before. My expectations for a close bond between my mother and myself were slim to none. I decided to leave it in God's hands and just let things unfold as they would.

We began interacting in a closer yet non-threatening manner. Phone calls were frequent and light-hearted. I tried to stay away from controversial topics. I have to admit I felt the grip of jealousy when my mother spent the bulk of our calls detailing every aspect of the daily lives of my sister and her children. During the next couple of years, I was surprised at the frequency my sister chose to connect with me also. It was like having a relationship with a stranger who knew considerable amounts of details about my life. We had a measure of polite correctness in every interaction we had and I continued exercising caution. Over the next months, the conversations with my mother began to move towards some deeper topics. I was always careful not to be the one to bring up the past, but I didn't hedge away from adding my thoughts and opinions whenever my mother chose to break the boundary she had set for us.

The first hurdle she chose to cross was not one I would have expected.

Out of the blue during a rather light chit chat we were having, she decided to tell me a joke. It had a Pentecostal man and some Catholics in it. We both laughed wholeheartedly at the punch line, after which my mother said, "Can you believe how stupid we were years ago?"

"What do you mean?" I asked.

God was pulling us together for the finale. It would be a miracle neither of us expected.

"You know," she said, "we all believe in Christ, and I'm no more a Christian than you are." I didn't know what to say. After more than twenty-five years, she was validating my faith. I felt a change in both of us that day. I knew she had started to re-evaluate what she had been thinking about me over the years and I had begun to do the same. God was pulling us together for the finale. It would be a miracle neither of us expected.

Chapter 12
/ I Honour You

*T*HINGS WERE BETTER now. Better, and yet that awful yearning for my mother to love me as much as my sister still haunted me. It was like a slow burning ember that was being fanned into flame every time I witnessed them interacting. Each conversation with my sister confirmed how close she and my mother had always been. I tried to resign myself to the fact that this was just the way it had to be, yet deep down I wanted and needed to know I mattered to her too—not just that she loved me because she gave birth to me. I had to know I held some special place in her heart that no one else did, even if it was just a small place.

More than five years had now passed, and I was feeling grateful that my daughters and husband had also reconciled with my mother. Angela and my mom were now having their own connection via phone conversations, and my mother loved to tell her stories about our visits when she was a baby and was always curious about the details of her love life. I began noticing a decline in my mother's health, which seemed to be getting worse as the weeks were passing. Her diabetes was raging and she seemed to be having a hard time getting it under control. I was pleasantly surprised when my mother, sister and brother-in-law arrived at my surprise fiftieth birthday party. This played a bigger role in the grand scheme of things, as this was the first time many of my friends had ever met my family and it was also the first time I grievously sensed God was beginning to close this chapter in my life. Deep down I just knew this would be our last year together.

> *Would I be one of those people who spent the remainder of their adult life on a therapist's couch because of unresolved issues about their mother?*

Part of me began to feel a sort of panic setting in. If she died now, how would I handle it? Would I be one of those people who spent the remainder of their adult life on a therapist's couch because of unresolved issues about their mother? Why would God bring me to this point and leave me dangling? I worked diligently at trying to put it out of my mind. Courtney was now engaged and we were in the thick of wedding plans, so that helped immensely. My mother and sister came up for her wedding shower, and when I saw my mother, all my worst fears were confirmed. I knew in my heart she was dying. I also realized, even if she lived to the time of the wedding, it was doubtful she would be able to make the trip. I began calling every few days for updates. It was at this time I noticed she began to delve into deeper topics with me whenever possible. I wondered if she sensed what was happening also.

The week before Mother's Day, my heart was breaking at the thought of what was ahead. It was now one month before Courtney's wedding and I was feeling very uneasy. Thoughts about the last six years and what had transpired seemed to be running around my mind like a never ceasing revolving door. I prayed God wouldn't let her suffer and that I would have the chance to see her again. It was at that moment I felt the Holy Spirit speak a truth into my life that, as difficult as it was to hear, I will forever be grateful for.

He said, *You are fifty years old and have never really honoured your mother.* That thought seemed to penetrate the deepest core of my soul. I began a mental struggle with God. Yes, perhaps I hadn't been everything a daughter should be, but I had called, remembered her birthday and sent gifts at Christmas. Wasn't that "honouring" her? I heard a resounding *NO* in my spirit. I knew it was true. Those were acts of obligation, not honour. To honour her would have meant to pay homage to the person she was, to look over her life and what she had endured and realize my life had been influenced by a woman who was a survivor. I had never held her in high regard for any part she played in my life or the lives of others. I also knew, no matter what had transpired through my life and the circumstances surrounding my relationship with my mother, if I professed to be a follower of Christ, I had to rectify this before she died. That evening I made the decision to follow that still small voice of conviction.

My husband and children had made reservations for brunch on Mother's Day. Normally we would have had lunch and then headed back to my home for an afternoon of visiting. This time, however, I told them I had decided to drive the four hours to Windsor right after lunch to be able to surprise my mom by spending the evening "honouring" her through Mother's Day dinner. I called my sister and asked her to set an extra place for dinner and to keep it a secret from our mother.

I left that day never imagining what was about to transpire. From the moment I kissed my husband goodbye and closed my car door, God surrounded me with an intense sense of purpose. It was as if those four hours would be spent allowing Him to prepare me for what was coming. For the first hour, my thoughts surrounded the wonderful lunch and time I had just spent with my own family. This Mother's Day seemed somehow different. During lunch I watched more closely than usual the way my husband, daughters, sons-in-law and my grandson interacted with each other. I looked at each of their faces individually and thanked God for the unique way they each brought joy to my life, hoping I had done the same for all of them. A strange thought ran through my mind. If I died today would they be able to say I loved them unconditionally? Had I made the toils of their lives seem lighter because of that?

My grandson had written me a letter for Mother's Day, touting all the things that made me special to him. At that moment he would never have known how meaningful and comforting this would be over the next week. Very much to my surprise, Angela, who was twenty-eight at the time, gave me a homemade card. She had dipped her hands in sparkly glue and put them on pink paper. It said, "Best Mother—Hands Down." She told me the children in her class had been making them for Mother's Day and since she was my little girl, she felt I should also have one. I laughed and the feeling I would get when she brought work home from school resurfaced out of my heart

> *If I died today would they be able to say I loved them unconditionally?*

as if it had been yesterday. I looked at the beautiful women my daughters had become and wondered where the time had gone.

A few miles passed and I began running through thoughts of what my mother would have been like as a child. I began to compile pieces of her life that I had heard stories about and lay them out in my mind like a giant puzzle. Her life hadn't been easy. Some of her childhood had been taken away when she had to quit school after grade eight to go to work. Her marriage to my father had caused problems with her parents, which must have accentuated the anguish of living with my dad's alcoholism and the enormous abnormality that plagued our family's relationships.

I began to cry when I had to admit that, even though I knew my father loved me more than life itself, there were times he had caused my mother enormous pain. She spent the bulk of her adult life working in a filthy factory in Detroit to help provide for us, and just when her life seemed to be turning around, she had to watch her husband die from cancer. I was hardly able to drive as remorse began to engulf me. I had never allowed myself to see the big picture. I then realized she had done the best with what she knew and had been dealt.

The actuality of our true life's journey began to fill my mind. The rejection I had felt from her and my sister was certainly real, but now I was also suffering from the reality of knowing I had built a wall of resentment that was so strong around me, it was impenetrable. Not even the slightest show of love and affection for her had been allowed past it. I asked God to forgive me for any way I had added to the mountain of grief she had suffered in her

I was hardly able to drive as remorse began to engulf me. I had never allowed myself to see the big picture.

lifetime. I asked to be relieved from any resentment I was holding towards her. I prayed for strength and wisdom. Time was running out and I needed this enormous void closed before it was too late.

I arrived at her home just before dinner. I parked down the street in case she was sitting in her living room. I wanted this to be a surprise. As I came closer, I heard the words my grandson had spoken on our first visit. *That's my grandma. She used to be your baby.*

As I reached for the doorknob, I heard God say, *Remember, your mother is My baby.*

At that moment I realized, more than ever before, God had carried both of us—"His babies"—our entire lives.

I slowly and quietly opened the door. I peeked in and spotted my sister. She motioned for me to be quiet and in a whisper told me my mom was in her bedroom getting something.

I crept down the hall and stood in the doorway to her bedroom. I will never in my lifetime forget the expression on her face when she looked up and saw me there. It's hard to describe. It wasn't just surprise, it was more like a joy unspeakable in the realization that she was experiencing something she would never have thought possible. It had been over thirty years since I had spent a Mother's Day with her.

She, of course, asked the obvious. "What are you doing here?"

I moved closer and said, "It's Mother's Day, and there's nowhere else I would rather be."

We hugged until neither of us could stand any longer. We went to the living room and the entire time we sat there waiting for dinner, she just kept looking at me, smiling, and shaking her head while exclaiming, "I can't believe you drove all this way to have dinner with me!" When I looked at her smile, I knew there really was nowhere else I would rather have been.

During dinner, my mother began exhibiting some awkward behaviour. She seemed almost detached at times. My sister thought perhaps her blood sugar was off. We spent most of the evening laughing, and for the first time I can ever remember, discussing my family seemed to be really important to her. I went to bed feeling I had accomplished what I had come for. After everyone was asleep, I sensed my mother was awake. I climbed into bed with her and we laughed and joked. She spent time discussing some serious issues that seemed to be plaguing her. It was as if she wanted to be sure I knew what was on her mind. She wasn't well but seemed somewhat relieved we had a chance to be alone.

I kissed her good night and went back to bed. This had now become my new "best day ever" with her. This was the first time I felt a closeness to her that was distinct, almost enlightening. I must have fallen into a deep sleep, for I didn't hear the commotion happening across the hall the next morning until my sister opened the bedroom door and said, "Come quick! I think Mom is having a heart attack or a stroke."

> *I kissed her good night and went back to bed. This had now become my new "best day ever" with her.*

I barely had time to think as I jumped up and ran to her bed. Something was drastically wrong. She was pale and obviously in pain. I lay on the bed with her as they called for an ambulance. She was coherent but seemed very weak. I tried to ask her what was wrong but she seemed confused. I was careful not to move in case it caused her pain, but I needed to look into her eyes. I perched over her and looked straight at her. She whispered, "Don't leave me. Just lay here."

I said, "Of course I will. Don't be afraid—God's with you. And I love you."

She squeezed my hand, smiled and said, "I love you too."

When the ambulance arrived, they had a difficult time getting information out of her. She was experiencing excruciating pain around her shoulder. Once they put her in the ambulance I felt relieved she would be on her way to the hospital. Surely they would stabilize her.

When I arrived at the hospital emergency, she seemed worse. They had to put an external pacemaker on her and were really perplexed about her shoulder pain. I gazed down at her and wondered why God would allow this now. I tried to run every scripture verse relevant to the situation through my mind for some comfort, but I was having a difficult time hearing them over the sound of my heart breaking. He had just given me a spectacular night with her, so why this? And why now? I was feeling somewhat alone.

The next few days were a blur. Feelings of grief were momentarily shadowed by thoughts she might rally around and get better. They informed us the pain she was experiencing in her shoulder was because it was dislocated. They were also having an arduous time getting her heart rate stabilized. She would require surgery and there was no guarantee it would end favourably. She was in and out of consciousness.

I went to her side and told her I was going home to get some things and would bring back my family to see her. I wondered if God would take her while I was gone. *Dear God,* I begged, *please keep her alive until I get back.* A strange calmness came over me, and I as I went closer to her to kiss her goodbye, she opened her eyes and said, "I'll wait for you."

I knew she would. I raced home, trying to make sense of everything as I drove. As I entered the house, seeing Michael gave me a renewed strength. I knew he had been covering me in prayer. We gathered our daughters the next morning and headed back. Fortunately, the girls kept my mind occupied during the trip. When we arrived, I felt anxious. Was she still here? Did she wait?

The relief at seeing her open her eyes nearly took my breath away. Even though she was weak, she was ever so happy to see Michael and the girls. At one moment, after Angela had been in to see her, my mother smiled and said, "She is so like you."

I made her laugh when I leaned in close to her and said, "Actually, the scary part is she might look like me, but really she's just like you!"

She was scheduled to have surgery that evening. I'm not exactly sure what conversation or action brought it on, but my resentment over her closeness towards my sister began to rear its ugly head with a vengeance. I was trying to comfort my sister any way I was able, but when she went into great detail to show me the forms she had to fill out to decide what measures would be taken or not taken to keep my mother alive, I was crushed all over again. Those feelings of not being as important as my sister were overtaking any love or attachment I had gained over the last few days. This would literally be the most important decision governing my mother's life, and it only involved my sister. The cavern of rejection in my heart had deepened by another blow.

My emotional turmoil escalated when, after the surgery, the doctor came to tell us they had fixed her shoulder as well as they were able and had put in the pacemaker. This should have been great news; however, when he began to make statements such as, "We would have normally done more extensive surgery and repair, but at this point we just tried to make her comfortable," I knew this was the end. We stayed until she came out of the anaesthetic and then they advised us to let her rest for the night. It was a night that seemed to have no end.

I awoke early the next morning. I felt empty. I felt cheated. My attempt to come to God in prayer seemed grossly inadequate. *God, I need You. Don't abandon me because of the resentment in my heart. Pease take it away so I can feel You.* I heard nothing. We arrived at the hospital and began taking turns going in and out of my mother's room. I began to see the stress and panic on my sister's face. I started to understand that, as traumatic as this was for me, it was devastating to her. She and my mother had practically been joined at the hip their entire lives, and now that relationship had the potential of being broken forever. It was the first time in my life I felt a sense of sorrow for her. *Dear God, help her,* I prayed. *Help her get through this.*

It was at that moment I found myself alone in the room with my mother. She was drifting in and out of consciousnesses. I began to beg God to help me. There were things I needed to know before she died or my life

> *I began to see the stress and panic on my sister's face. I started to understand that, as traumatic as this was for me, it was devastating to her.*

would forever be incomplete. Did she know I really loved her? That I never meant to hurt her? Did she know how I had longed for her touch as a child—not just a hug or a pat on the head, but a sweet tender touch that made me know there was a special place in her heart that was only for me?

Dear God, does she know? Don't leave me wondering.

Then it happened. It was the miracle I had waited for my entire life. I saw my mother awaken. She motioned with her hand for me to come near. As I approached her bed, I felt God draw near to both of us. It was as if He had His hands outstretched, touching both of us at the same time. When I reached her side she became unusually alert, and as I gazed into her eyes she said, "I do know," after which she took my hand, closed her eyes and kissed my fingers with a deep, intense yet tender touch. It was the type of endearing kiss only a mother that deeply loves her child is capable of.

God had spoken to both of us. He had mended the void in both of our hearts. We were, at that moment, a mother and daughter who loved each other unconditionally. I kissed her cheek and she told me there were times I had brought her great joy. She thanked me for giving her Angela and told me how proud she was to see her settled in her new life. She mentioned how special Michael, Tracy and Courtney were to her. I was given instructions to give Mackenzie a big fat kiss, and she told me she would keep an eye on him from Heaven. I began to cry but she told me to stop. Calmly and confidently she said, "There's nothing more we need to say; Jesus will take care of both of us. Now, listen carefully. I want you take Michael and the girls and go home. No more long conversations between us. I love you."

Then it happened. It was the miracle I had waited for my entire life.

"I love you too, Mom."

I understood what was happening. We had experienced the greatest moment we would ever have together and we needed nothing more. On the other hand, because of the relationship she had always had with my sister, it was important they be alone together when she died. Oddly enough, I was fine with that. We all said our goodbyes and left for home. Once home, I felt exhausted and saddened but my heart was full. Michael asked me how I was feeling, and I told him my prayer was that she wouldn't suffer and that God would take her peacefully. I walked down to my bedroom as the phone rang. I heard Michael say, "OK, just a minute."

It was my sister, her voice trembling. "Mom is gone, Mary Anne. She said her prayers and that was it." We talked for a moment and I hung up the phone. I began to cry, which then turned to sobbing to help release the pain. After a few moments passed, I remember thinking, *Even though she's gone, I'll always be her baby.*

Chapter 13
/ The End, My Beginning

He who began a good work in you
will carry it on to completion. *

HERE WAS A time in my life when I considered this verse an overall commentary of God's perfect plan for our lives: very simply stated, they have a beginning and an end. I have since come to the conclusion that this isn't completely accurate. Life isn't just a journey of starting a good work and following it through to that great climax of completion. It's actually a series of completions He helps us through, and should we chose to make *His* desire for us our desire, then each completion provides an insight into His goodness, mercy, grace and love.

Writing this book gave me the opportunity to really take a deep look at the pieces of the experiences that have brought me to where I am today. In times past I would look at a person's life and destructive behaviour and excuse them because I felt they were victims of their upbringing or

---

* Philippians 1:6

horrific acts that had been perpetrated on them as children. I nurtured the thought that somehow this gave them license to continue perpetuating that same behaviour generation after generation. That was until I saw the curse of destruction manifesting itself in my own life and realized I would need to take a stand to break that chain. I would need to become the victor, not the victim. It wasn't easy, because with that realization came the guilt and remorse of knowing that even though I, too, was a victim of my circumstances. Some of the destruction in my own life was because I had walked through the dark waters of my own indulgence. Resentment, hate and unforgiveness became comfortable. I owed it to myself, or so I thought.

> *Some of the destruction in my own life was because I had walked through the dark waters of my own indulgence. Resentment, hate and unforgiveness became comfortable.*

Looking back over these fifty-plus years, I now see the clear markings of the eras of completion I have come through. The hurt and pain that wove its way into the pattern of my life was never part of God's plan; however, He gave me the strength to endure it to the end of its time, its completion. As each season came to an end, it served only as another step to bring me closer to Him and the unveiling of His greater plan. I was learning to make His desires for me my desires.

I can't help but think back to when Michael and I were in Hawaii and visited the volcano park. We heard the story of how years ago the volcano erupted and molten hot lava crept its way across several miles of what was beautiful Eden-like countryside and literally destroyed everything that lay in its path. Once it had cooled down, only devastation and hardened black ash remained. I remember looking out at the blackness of the ground and feeling an almost evil intention there. That was before I noticed in several isolated spots some plants had begun to grow right out of the ash. I remember thinking this was a great testimony to God's goodness. It truly was beauty from ashes. I now know this is also the testimony of God's goodness in my life.

I started my life as beautiful and pristine as that countryside in Hawaii, but then darkness covered me with the intent of keeping me covered and keeping me in such a state that anyone looking over my life would never have considered the beauty that would rise out of it. Slowly, and not without my own resistance, God's grace and strength began to push me upwards. I first broke through the ash with the strength that came from forgiveness—not only towards others but also towards myself. I then began to see the beautiful light that came from compassion and the conscious decision not to judge others. More grace and a greater sense of completion followed. Now I was at the place of being exposed for the entire world to see. Yes, beauty from ashes.

At this stage of completion, I was experiencing a heart-gripping sense of conviction that grew into a steadfast mindset. In order for me to stand strong in God's abiding love, I would now have to see beauty in others through His eyes, especially those who were unable to see it in themselves. I no longer possessed the option to choose or differentiate between those I wanted to be with and love and those I felt no attraction towards. It would now be a fulfilling honour to show His love and kindness to anyone He chose to put in my path. I was daily moving closer to experiencing the awareness of His never ending presence in my life. I was moving towards the closure of the most intense chapter of my life.

My mother's death and the circumstances that surrounded that day moved me to a greater sense of just how in control of my life God actually is. It was a full demonstration of the supernatural benefits available to any person willing to give Christ a place in their heart and life. It was the end—and the beginning.

> *In order for me to stand strong in God's abiding love, I would now have to see beauty in others through His eyes, especially those who were unable to see it in themselves.*

It was the end of the resentment and consuming pain of rejection. God supernaturally healed the hurts from our past and filled our hearts with a complete love for each other. For the first time in my life, I felt a peace about my mother that surpassed anything I had felt before. God knew I would never have allowed myself total freedom in life without bringing closure to the events of my childhood experiences.

He can do the same for you. If you are reading this and are imprisoned by the hold of a past that continually invades your present, you can be free. Let Jesus take you by the hand and lead you along the first steps towards completion. If you let Him, He will make that ending your greatest beginning.

Chapter 14
/ The True Measure of Change

WHILE WRITING THIS book, I began to wonder what my daughters would say about me once I was gone. I knew I loved them beyond measure, but had I really made any difference in their lives or was the chain of inadequate relationships being perpetuated?

I know I have been fortunate to experience love from the positions of both birth mother and stepmother, but the measure of my life as a mother will be whether these women found love and acceptance unconditionally from me. I decided the only way to know would be to ask them, for there could be no more fitting to end this book than to see if they felt the true measure of change.

Here are their thoughts:

Tracy

My mom—where do I begin? We met when I was eight years old and finally, when I was ten, she married my dad.

The woman I am referring to as "Mom" may not have given birth to me, but that hasn't made her any less of a mother or made me feel any less of a daughter because that's exactly what we are in the true sense of the words: Mother and Daughter.

Over the years, my mom has nurtured me into the woman I am today and for that I will always be grateful. She is the most understanding, intelligent, compassionate woman I know. Faith, morals and family values are just some of the traits she instilled in us. We always went to church every Sunday as we were growing up and, like many children, we found it boring. My mom would tell us it was important to go, and considering all that God provided for us twenty-four hours a day, it was only an hour of our time we were giving up, so that really wasn't too much to ask. It wasn't until I was twenty-three and experiencing an extremely difficult time in my life that I truly understood why she taught us faith was so important.

We were always able to see the spiritual bond my parents had with God and what affect that had, not only on their relationship with each other, but also on those around them. She always taught us that God's love is unconditional and that no matter how many times we turn our back on Him, He's always there to catch us when we fall.

Whether you find her in the kitchen or just hanging around the house, my mother is one of the most creative people I know. When I look at myself now as a wife and mother, I'm happy to say I picked up some of those traits. My love for baking was stirred primarily out of our special relationship. For as long as I can remember, Mom was always baking away for all of us, and when I was younger I loved to sit and watch. I learned a great deal from her, as she was always eager to let me pitch in. She was never afraid I would ruin the Christmas pie or the birthday cake she was making for Dad. Instead, she seemed proud to have me as her helper.

Most importantly, my mother has never turned her back on me, even when we didn't always agree. She has always provided a shoulder to cry on and a smile to laugh with.

She's never judgemental, but offers great suggestions when needed. I can honestly say I would not be the person I am today without my mom's direction, thoughtfulness, insight and unconditional love. I love you, Mom.

Courtney

My mom has taught me some great things in life. She has shown me the importance of loving your family, faith in God and the toughest one for me—patience. She also always kept reminding us to have complete trust in God, for He had a reason for allowing us to go through challenges some of the time. I can still hear her: "Seek God's word first in every decision and peace will surely follow."

I can't describe how fortunate I have been to have grown up in a house where love and support were always shown. I have so many wonderful memories from my childhood. After my parents divorced and my dad decided to re-marry, I can honestly say I set out to give his new wife as hard a time as I was able! The most frustrating part of this for me was her patience. No matter what tantrum I pulled or what terrible behaviour I exhibited, she always told me she loved me. Finally, I had to give up—she won me over. From the day they got married until now, she has always shown me just how much she is capable of loving me. Even though she isn't my biological mother, she has never treated me any differently. She has always assured me she is my mother and will always love me as if I were her own.

"Seek God's word first in every decision and peace will surely follow."

Because of my mom, I am excited to be in my new life with my husband and hopefully starting our own family where we can also teach them how to love and respect each other.

Mom has given me a lot of guidance over the years in many aspects of my life. She has always tried to make it practical. As mentioned before, patience isn't exactly one of my stronger virtues. (I'm really not sure how she has so much of it!) I remember driving with her one day when my perpetual habit of being frustrated with everyone around me was flourishing. I was yelling at people for not signalling or driving too slow or not seeming to know where they were going. I could see her smiling, and she calmly said, "You might want to try to have a little more patience with those people in front of you because we just can't be sure what might be going on in their lives right now. Maybe something has happened. For all we know, one of their family members may be in the hospital fighting for their life, and they're just distracted."

That one short lesson really made me reassess how I look at other people. Now that I think of it, that's the way she has always taught us. One short lesson at a time eventually changes your life. Mom, I love you.

Angela

When my mother asked me to write a section for her book, she said, "It doesn't have to be long. Just talk about our relationship and some of things you learned from me."

No problem, I thought. Then I tried to prioritize all the important "life lessons" she has taught me over the years. Which ones should I talk about? Were there some I felt were more important to share with the world than others? I began to think maybe this writing thing wouldn't be so easy after all. I sat there staring at a blank screen, and then it hit me. All of this, our relationship and what she's taught me, can be summed up with one simple word: EVERYTHING.

What have I learned from her?…EVERYTHING.

What has she taught me?…EVERYTHING.

What does our mother/daughter relationship mean to me? …EVERYTHING.

Ever since I can remember—especially in my early years—it has been my mom and I against the world: a team, and the best of friends. It's hard for me to explain my relationship with my mom in only a few short sentences, and really, I'm not sure I can "describe" it at all. Not with words, anyway. She has been the only constant in my life, no matter what. Even though I am happily married and have great friends and family, my mother and our relationship is certainly something I will never doubt. She is so many things to me I don't know where to begin.

Growing up, she always made me, our relationship and our family her number one priorities. I think, because her family life growing up was so awful, she was determined to make sure this didn't happen again. And it didn't. I was very young when my parents divorced; so young, in fact, I don't even have any memories of them having been together.

So now, imagine yourself in my mother's position: young, single mother going through a nasty divorce, living alone in a strange city with a low paying job, no family support and probably at this time minimal friends. Anyone in her position would probably call this rock bottom. I've had people say, "That must have been so hard on you, Angela, being so little and going through all that." And I agree. I'm sure for most kids that would be enough to scar you for life, but the truth be told, I barely remember it.

Well, I remember it—not as a bad time, but as a great time, actually—and that's because of my mother. She has always been like a phoenix, rising from the ashes, no keeping her down. She could have given up, quit her job and moved back home, but that would have been a quick fix for her, the easy way out. In her mind (and like always), it wasn't about her and her life and what she wanted, it was about me and what I *needed*. She used to bake desserts at home and sell them to a restaurant, that's how we survived. I don't remember struggling or having less things than other kids. There didn't seem to be hard times and I don't ever remember being unhappy. All I remember is a little girl who got to spend every waking moment with her mother, playing, singing and baking. I even used to go on deliveries with her. She knew her priorities and did what she needed to do, not what was easiest for her, and I thank God for that everyday. I honestly believe that it was those moments and decisions that not only made our relationship what it is, but also influenced the woman I am today, which I hope…is just like my mom.

Describing my relationship with my mother as "special" or "important" would be almost insulting because it's much more than that. I've moulded my entire life around her, our love for each other and everything she's taught me—and why wouldn't I? She's the closest thing to perfection I have ever seen. I can only pray that someday I might be half the woman, wife and mother that she is.

If you know anything about my mother, you'll know she is much more normal than she should have been allowed to be. She has survived through life's unfortunate circumstances and that just shows you the special type of person she is. They say, "When life gives you lemons, make lemonade." Well, she made lemonade alright … and tarts, and pies and loaves (sometimes literally!). Aside from being the world's greatest mother and wife, she is so much more to so many people, especially me. I hardly make a decision without consulting her first. She is so knowledgeable about so many things and I don't think she realizes the impact she has on others. She changes people's lives, and always for the better. I should know, I've seen and lived it. She's a teacher, a leader, an absolute inspiration and my own real life guardian angel. She's almost like having a twin. You know—that one person who understands and gets you, no questions asked.

I hope the point I am trying to make in this piece is as obvious to others as it is to me. I absolutely love and adore my mother with every fibre of my being. I don't just owe her my life's happiness, she is one of the most integral parts of my life. I hope everyone in this world can experience a bond like the one we have at least once in their life. It's relationships like the one I have with my mother that make life worth living because, God knows, I can't imagine life without her.

I love you, Mom, a bushel and a peck, and a hug around the neck.

THE TRUE MEASURE OF CHANGE